Christian Convention, Dwight L. Moody

Sermons and Addresses

Question Drawer and Other Proceedings of the Christian Convention Held in

Chicago, September 18th to 20th, 1883

Christian Convention, Dwight L. Moody

Sermons and Addresses

Question Drawer and Other Proceedings of the Christian Convention Held in Chicago, September 18th to 20th, 1883

ISBN/EAN: 9783337158903

Printed in Europe, USA, Canada, Australia, Japan

Cover: Foto ©Lupo / pixelio.de

More available books at **www.hansebooks.com**

FARWELL HALL, CHICAGO.

SERMONS & ADDRESSES

QUESTION DRAWER,

AND

OTHER PROCEEDINGS

OF THE

CHRISTIAN CONVENTION

HELD IN CHICAGO, SEPTEMBER 18TH TO 20TH, 1883.

UNDER THE DIRECTION OF

D. L. MOODY.

Verbatim Rerorts Carefully Revised.

CHICAGO:
FAIRBANKS, PALMER & CO.
1884.

CHAS. N. TRIVESS, PRINTER,
CHICAGO.

PREFACE

Among all those, from Paul to the devout of our own day, who can truthfully say: "I determined to know nothing among you save Jesus Christ and Him crucified," few have succeeded so well in singleness of purpose and strength of faith as Mr. Moody. Through no self-assertion he has come to occupy a prominence which would gratify the most high vaulting ambition; but no man could be freer than he from ambition, as a motive power. His whole heart is in the work of saving souls. In the vineyard of the Lord there are other labors to be performed, apart from the direct work of personal evangelization, but it must be conceded that he has "chosen the better part," and is engaged in the noblest work on earth.

However large his audiences and frequent his discourses, Mr. Moody can reach only a very few people, comparatively, and out of his zeal for the conversion of sinners has flown a stream of influence upon all evangelical churches in which the English language is spoken. The importance of this stream God alone can measure. Thanks to the printing press, he may address millions. And it is to the credit of the Christian ministry, and of the lay piety of all our churches, that there is a very general anxiety to feel the inspiration of his magnetic zeal, and to emulate his spirit and methods, so far as practicable and possible. The Pharasaical spirit which sneeringly asks: "How knoweth this man letters, having never learned?" is not manifested. On the contrary, the most learned of our ministry delight to sit at his feet, and the most eloquent gladly take lessons from him in that oratory which wins souls to Christ. The phenomenal favor with which Mr. Moody and his work have been received on both sides of the Atlantic will stand in the history of Christianity as monumental evidence of the humble piety and high devotion of the period. The fact that this book has now reached the twentieth edition, with an accelerated demand, is only one of the many evidences of this most encouraging state of the church.

The Christian Convention, which met in Chicago, September 18, 1883, remaining in session three days, was the immediate occasion of this latest, but not last, edition of MOODY'S SERMONS. The material furnished by those proceedings will be found to be of the very deepest interest and most vital importance, including not only Mr. Moody's sermons, and less formal, but not less valuable remarks, but also the addresses, brief and pithy, often sublimely eloquent and always appropriate, of other Christians of eminence in the work of saving souls. The varied experiences of many workers in independent vineyards, under widely diverse circumstances, brought out a flood of light such as few occasions and books could possibly focalize. It was by no means a one-man convention. Mr. Moody was surrounded and assisted by pastors and lay preachers upon whose labors the Master has impressed the signet of his approval by the ingathering of souls and the upbuilding of His church.

The publishers are indebted for the report of these meetings, to the journalistic enterprise of "*The Inter-Ocean.*" It was found unnecessary to have a corps of our own reporters present for that work, as it was being done to meet the immediate demands of the newspaper public. The benefit of this economy, in the cost of the twentieth edition, is given entirely to the public, as the edition is sold for the same price as the old and smaller one.

It is well known that newspapers aim to publish what their readers want, and the fact that a great daily journal in the eminently busy city of Chicago, should devote two pages a day to the proceedings of the Christian Convention, is a deeply significant attestation of the general interest taken in the proceedings. Not only the religious element of the city took a profound interest in them, but thousands of ministers and laymen from without, came to Chicago for the sole purpose of attending the meetings. Could they have been held in the Tabernacle, made sacred by the great revival meetings of a few years ago, the reports of which are given in this volume, it would have been crowded to overflow. But that temporary structure long since disappeared, and Farwell Hall, with its hallowed associations, afforded the best attainable accommodations.

Those who did not enjoy the holy luxury of attending the meetings and those who did, will alike find the report of those proceedings most suggestive reading, rich in seeds of thought and incentives to religious endeavor, at once intensely spiritual and thoroughly practical.

CONTENTS.

MORNING SERMON, SEPT. 16, 1883, BY D. L. Moody	866
EVENING " " " " " "	875
HOW CAN WE BEST SECURE A PREPARATION FOR CHRIST'S WORK, Rev. E. P. Goodwin, D. D.	890
SAME SUBJECT CONTINUED, Major D. W. Whittle	892
" " " H. L. A. Stevenson.	893
" " " D. L. Moody	893
THE GREAT HINDRANCES, Rev. J. H. Barrows, D. D.	895
" " " " C. L. Goodell, D. D.	901
" " " " D. L. Moody	902
QUESTION DRAWER, CONDUCTED BY D. L. Moody	905
HOW TO INTEREST THE LAY ELEMENT OF OUR CHURCHES Rev. C. L. Goodell, D. D.	909
HOW FAITH SPREADS, Rev. S. J. McPherson	914
QUESTION DRAWER, CONDUCTED BY D. L. Moody	918
HOW TO REACH HABITUAL NON-CHURCH GOERS, Rev. H. M. Scudder, D. D.	923
SAME, SUBJECT CONTINUED, Rev. M. M. Parkhurst	929
" " " Rt. Rev. C. E. Cheney, D. D.	931
WHAT SHALL BE DONE TO SECURE A MORE GENERAL ATTENDANCE OF THE PEOPLE UPON WORSHIP, Rev. P. S. Henson, D. D.	933
SAME SUBJECT CONTINUED, J. L. Houghteling	937
HOW CAN THE INFLUENCE OF CHRISTIAN HOMES BE INCREASED, Rev. Dr. Ninde	940
SAME SUBJECT CONTINUED, Rev. R. M. Hatfield D. D.	941

i.

CONTENTS.

DEVOTIONAL EXERCISES, Rev. W. M. Lawrence, D. D.	944
" " Charles M. Morton	947
METHODS OF ORGANIZATION FOR RELIGIOUS WORK, William Reynolds	948
QUESTION DRAWER, CONDUCTED BY D. L. Moody	951
SERMON. TEXT IN TITUS 2; 11–14, D. L. Moody	955
HOW CAN THE PERSONAL AND SOCIAL STUDY OF THE BIBLE BE INCREASED, Rev. Herrick Johnson, D. D.	969
SAME SUBJECT CONTINUED, B. F. Jacobs	974
HOW MAY OUR FOREIGN POPULATION BE EVANGELIZED, Rev. F. E. Emerich	975
HOW TO REACH THE GERMANS, Rev. L. M. Heilman	977
" " " " Prof. Samuel Ives Curtiss	980
HOW SHALL WE INTEREST OUR CHILDREN IN THE GOSPEL, Rev. E. C. Ray	988
HOW MAY MUSIC BE BEST USED AND CONTROLLED IN PROMOTING WORSHIP AND SPREADING THE GOSPEL, Ira D. Sankey	993
SAME SUBJECT CONTINUED, James McGranahan	998
" " " D. L. Moody	1005
" " " Rev. P. S. Henson, D. D.	1006
" " " Rev. Herrick Johnson, D. D.	1007
CLOSING ADDRESSES ON "CONSECRATION FOR THE WORK," Rev. E. P. Goodwin, D. D.	1008
SAME SUBJECT CONTINUED, William Reynolds, Prof. Morehead, Mr. Lattimer, Rev. Dr. Hatfield, J. S. Smithson, Major D. W. Whittle, Bishop Cheney, Rev. Dr. Henson, and others.	
CLOSING ADDRESS BY D. L. Moody.	1010

CHRISTIAN CONVENTION.

HELD AT FARWELL HALL, CHICAGO, SEPTEMBER 18, 19 AND 20, 1883. PREFACED BY THE TWO SERMONS PREACHED BY MR. MOODY THE SUNDAY PREVIOUS. PROCEEDINGS AND SERMONS REPORTED IN FULL.

MORNING SERVICE. SEPT. 16, 1883.

For the first time for many years, D. L. Moody, Chicago's own great evangelist, appeared on a pulpit platform in that city, where he grew into greatness. The mere announcement that the great evangelist was to preach at the Chicago Avenue Church was sufficient to secure the filling of that church many times over. Long before the doors of the church were open, dense crowds covered the sidewalks on the two street sides of the church.

After the opening services Mr. Moody made a few remarks relative to that particular church, before entering upon the theme of the occasion.

MOODY'S CHURCH.

You are all aware that this is a free church. I see some of you putting your hands in your pockets, seeing what I am coming at. A good many of my friends said to me that this church could not succeed, because it was an undenominational church; because it was not a Baptist, or a Methodist, or a Presbyterian church; that no undenominational church could live. Well, it has lived now for twenty years, and, while I am no prophet, I think it will live twenty years longer. My heart has been wonderfully cheered that I have not had to raise any money this time to pay pastors' bills. Everything is paid up to the present time, and I believe the true Scriptural idea of a church is that every one should give as he is prospered from day to day and week to week. We don't ask you to give what you haven't got, but we want you to give this morning as you have been blessed in worldly store. There is one thing that should be remedied at once—the sidewalk on Chicago avenue in front of the church. I almost feared the crowd this morning would break it down, and I should like to have a stone sidewalk put there instead of the old wooden one. We need $2,000 for this, and that is not much for a congregation like this so there will be no danger of the sidewalk breaking in and the people getting hurt. So we will devote to that purpose the collection both this morning and evening.

THE MORNING SERMON.

I have, said Mr. Moody, four texts this morning. One is a question, another is an exhortation, another is a command, and the last, the fourth, is a promise.

And, first, the question: It is the first words that fell from the lips of Christ as recorded by John. Other evangelists record other words, but these are the first recorded by John, "What seek ye?" According to the commentators, John wrote the Gospel about sixty years after Christ was gone, the last New Testament book written, and he was so impressed with the interview he held with Christ that it figures in his opening sentence. It was in the afternoon on the day after John had been baptized. On seeing the Saviour in the presence of His disciples, John cried out, "Behold the Lamb of God!" And John followed Jesus, and Jesus turned to John and his accompanying disciples and said, "What seek ye?"

Now, all classes sought the Lord when He was on earth, the rich and poor, the learned and the unlearned; there was not a class to stay away; the priests and the Levites, the Pharisees and the Sadducees, all classes sought Him. But they didn't all seek Him with the same motive, and therefore they didn't all get blessed alike.

Some sought Him that they might see a sign. They wanted to see Him perform a miracle. They wanted to see a man lame from his birth jump up and walk, and see him leaping and praising God. That's a sight they'd like to see. They didn't care anything about the explanation. They only wanted the excitement of the spectacle. Some were a little skeptical and didn't believe. But they didn't come there to believe; they didn't want to believe. And so they were constantly coming to see a sign. And one day He turned Him to them and asked them the question of the text. We can imagine that these men spread the reports of what they saw all over Palestine.

It was a great wonder, indeed, that here was one who could make bread without flour. It was a marvel, truly, that He could give them food in the desert without any preparation, the very best bread that ever they had eaten. Fresh from the hand of the Creator, of course it was good bread. They didn't care about anything else, except to say that they had seen and tasted it. Just so nowadays; some men rush to hear somebody preach to just be able to say that they have heard him. They don't care what he says, but they love to say, "Oh, yes, I have seen him and heard him." And so there was that class of men who sought Him.

And others sought Him because they thought He was going to set up a temporal kingdom, and they would be the first in authority under Him—wanted to be prime ministers and secretaries of state, and all that, monopolizing all the fat offices of the land. I have not any doubt that such was the motive that took Judas into the ranks of the Lord; he wanted high position, the fishes and loaves of worldly prominence and lordship. The same class existed then as now, and with the same motive; they followed the Lord because it promised rewards of an earthly kind, and to be His disciple would be the fashion.

Another class sought Him that they might entangle Him in His conversations, that they might accuse him before the law, and take Him out and stone Him to death. They wanted to get something against Him. They wanted to trap Him into some utterance against Cæsar. They had nothing but murder in their hearts. Others sought Him because the crowd went that way, for multitudes were going into the desert to see the signs and the wonders that were wrought. Many went because others went, and if they answered truly the question, "What seek ye?" they would have answered, "I am going to see what is going on." Another class wanted to hear some new thing. They would like to hear this new doctrine. And there was another class that didn't care. They were ready to take in anything that was going on.

And another class—and I am sorry to say that is a small class—sought Him for what He was. And let me say right here that no man or woman was ever disappointed. Christ is all, and more than we make Him to be. Men grow smaller and smaller, but don't grow larger and larger. No man ever made too much of Christ Jesus. Some people have a very small Savior, and are continually venturing into sin. Why? Because they do not know the power of that Savior, have no intimate acquaintance with Christ, don't know much about Him. But when he is the great and mighty Savior, and recognized in the soul as such, then a man's path is safe.

And now let me look into this audience this morning and let me ask the question, What seek ye? and answer me truly. The text is not changed. It is the same to-day as when Christ uttered it, and is man changed? Not one bit. I think if this audience could be sifted and you could get at the reasons that brought people together this morning you would find much similarity to the old reasons. Hundreds of men and women came here this morning who did not come to learn. It is the hardest thing in the world to reach such. I believe hundreds and thousands of people go to church Sabbath after Sabbath, and go away without one thought of duty upon them, just as untouched as for the last twenty years. They did not come to the house of God to meet God, they do not bring their souls into contact with the grace of Christ.

Now all are seeking for something, and let the question come,

What seek ye? Come, friends, ask the question of yourselves. What was your motive in coming here this morning? Did some come for information? "I just came," you say, "to see what was going on. I was going down street this morning and saw the great crowd and thought I would just come in and hear what was going on." You have just dropped in. Well, glad you are here, and if you haven't come with the best motive I hope God will meet you.

Another, perhaps, has come in order to please his mother. "She has been very anxious," you say, "that I should come out to meeting, and I thought it would please her." Well, I am glad you have come, even if you didn't come with a better motive than that.

On my last visit to London I was preaching in Agricultural Hall when a man dropped in out of the rain, and he staid till he found the Savior. Well, I was reminded of Sir Rowland Hill, who said that he had heard of people making a cloak out of religion, but this man made an umbrella out of it. [Laughter.] Another time a man dropped in who said he hadn't been in a church before for years. This was in Philadelphia where I was speaking one Tuesday night. He was a bricklayer, a great strapping six-footer, a hard-drinking man, and very profane. Well, somebody had told him it was a remarkable sight to see 11,000 empty chairs on one floor, and he thought he would like to see them. Didn't care for the Gospel, but wanted to see the empty tabernacle and those chairs. Low motive, wasn't it? So, early in the evening he came up, and as soon as the sexton unlocked the door he popped in ahead of everybody, and ran up the aisle to see the empty chairs from the foreground. He said: "What do so many fools rush in here for?" But he stayed, and the divine word and Holy Spirit began to tell on him, and he has adorned the doctrine of God his Savior ever since. That's the kind of people to preach to. They are open to God's truth. I would rather preach to that kind than those who become hardened under pulpit ministrations. Those are the hardest to reach.

If you have heard the word unmoved and disobedient, I don't think there is much chance for you. God in His mercy may save you, but there is not much hope for you. However, come ahead; even if like that bricklayer you haven't come with the best of motives. Our God is a great God, and He is able to bless every one, and he knows our needs better than any one. So let us pray God that every one may seek His face and find Him precious.

The next text tells us to "Seek the Lord while He may be found." Now notice how it reads: "Seek the Lord while He may be found." It does not say seek happiness, seek peace, seek joy. And yet a good many people are only seeking these; seeking peace, seeking joy, seeking happiness. I cannot see any place in the Bible where we are told to seek for peace, for happiness, for joy. If we seek after the virtue, we will have all those things following. If we have the spirit we will have the fruit. We cannot get an apple without we have the tree. We cannot have an orange without we have an orange tree. Set a good tree and you will have good fruit. Therefore, what is wanted is to seek the Lord Himself. If we get the Lord we will have peace, joy, rest. We cannot have them without Christ. Christ Himself comes with them; brings them to us. He is the author and bearer of them. If we want peace, therefore, and joy and happiness, and rest, we must seek Him.

Call upon him while he is near.

I remember, when I was a boy, a little fellow, smaller than this boy here, I would try—you may think I was a foolish fellow—I would try to catch my shadow. But many a time I have tried to tread on my shadow, but I never caught my shadow. I would run after it a good many times, but never caught up with it. But once, running toward the sun, I saw my shadow coming after me; and one of the sweetest lessons I have learned in the school of righteousness is, and was, that the fruit comes after our seeking the Lord. Make the tree good, and the fruit will be good. Seek Him and we have all the hope, the peace, the rest, and happiness that we desire. Now, dear friends, if we seek these things instead of seeking Christ, we shall be disappointed.

Do you think the Lord can be found in this house before twelve o'clock? Can a man who has been living in sin up to this hour, who has never sought the Lord until this hour, do you believe that such a man can see Him within this house, before twelve o'clock? Yes! I believe it, just as much as I believe in anything. If there is any man who cannot find Him, I believe it is because he does nothing to find Him; and the reason that so few people find the Lord is because they do not seek Him in their heart. They cannot find Him in the head. The seeking after the Lord is the work of revelation, and revelation comes to the heart and not to the head of man. When people seek God from the heart they find Him. When I said to another man that I could tell him when he would be converted, he answered: "Mr. Moody, I did not know that you claimed to be a prophet." I said that I was not a prophet, nor my father before me. If men will be earnest in their souls they need not go out of the house to find Him.

His salvation is within the reach of every soul here if he will wake up as the man did on the day of Pentecost. The cry was, "What must we do?" And when He told them, they went and bowed themselves down. And if you are willing to do what God wants you to do, and seek Him with all your heart, you will find Him. Once, at one of my meetings, a man was leaning upon a post with both his hands in his pockets. "Are you a Christian, friend?"

I asked. He said, "No!" "Would you like to be one?" "I have no objection," he replied. Now, I don't think that man is fit to be saved with that kind of a spirit, and I do not believe that any man will ever step into the kingdom of God in that condition of mind. If people were as anxious about their eternal welfare as they are about their temporal welfare, there would be no trouble to men and women getting into the kingdom of God by hundreds.

People are so earnestly bent on their temporal affairs, so diligent and self-sacrificing in piling up earthly riches, that they have softening of the brain, so much are they troubled in reference to that which perisheth. They are terribly in earnest about these things which are earthly and which perish. Shall we not be in earnest about the things eternal? It is no time to seek God when the house begins to fall, when the walls are coming down, when we are tortured on the bed of sickness. It is no time then to seek eternal riches. It is this beautiful Sabbath morning, this very hour, that we should call upon Him while He is near.

Is He near? That is the question of many. If any man or woman thinks He is far away, let them remember that He said that when only "two of you are together, I am with you." Is He not still merciful? Is He not still gracious? Does He not still want to lift up the world? Does He not wish to place you on the heights above? Did God not show His love for us when He sent His only begotten Son down into this world for our salvation, when He left the throne and came down into this dark world, and passed by the columns of the palace and went to the manger? Was he not in earnest? And, dear friends, if God was in earnest when He came among us to die on the cross, shall we not be in earnest? Is it not time to turn toward Him—to seek the Lord when He may be called?

The text shows that the time has come. There are many that have called when it was too late.

Now take the third section of my text, and that is a command: "Seek first the kingdom of God, and His righteousness, and all these things shall be added unto you." Now, if that means what it says, and I have no doubt it does, it means to seek the kingdom of God before you go out of this house this morning. It means you are to seek Him before you go home—before you take another step. There is not a thing that you can put between your salvation and your soul—no solitary thing. No man or woman in this place ought to think of waiting for a moment. You know that all of God's blessings have come that way. Take the life of Christ while He was here, and its one teaching is, be obedient.

Every solitary one who did what he thought he ought to do was blessed. Take blind Bartimeus who was commanded to go his way, and he went and was blessed in the very act of going. To another this blessed Lord said, "Go home and tell your friends what great things the Lord has done." He started home and he was blessed on the way. He said to the ten lepers, "Go show yourselves to the priests!" These men might have said, "We show ourselves to the priests! Why they have banished us to the desert, sent us outside the walls of the city, crying 'Unclean! unclean!'" But the ten obeyed, and what was the result? They were healed in the very act of obedience. I would like to have seen those ten men who were healed, as their wholeness dawned upon them. "Why, look here, John, I am whole; I feel as if I could leap over a stone wall." And another says, "So am I," and the whole ten find that they are whole, and walk and leap and praise God.

And you remember the paralytic to whom the word came, "Take up thy bed and walk." He did not withhold obedience one second, and God gave him power to fulfill the word. So you can always take God at his word, and in obedience to your salvation. What he has commanded He will give you ability to perform. Obedience, that is the first and great thing. No other question will compare with that of our immortal destiny.

I can imagine the commotion there would be in this audience this morning if a whisper should go through the congregation, "Solomon is here." How all eyes would turn to yonder door in wondering expectancy. And if he should walk to the platform, how hushed you would be. I can imagine you would look up to him in reverence and love. I can imagine his saying to you, "Whatsoever thy hand findeth to do, do it with thy might, for there is no knowledge in the grave whither thou goest." Do what thou hast to do with all thy might. My friends—is there any other question of importance to compare with this question of eternal life?

To buy and sell, to get gain, and live a little longer in Chicago—is that so important as this question of eternal life? Suppose you had rolled up the wealth of Crœsus, and had not eternal life; suppose you should live many years longer without eternal life; is there anything in this life compared with the life beyond?

And I imagine another speaker coming in. He is the old prophet of Carmel, the Tishbite. Wouldn't you like to hear Elijah? He has got a strange coat on, all camel's hair, walks like a giant. You say, "I would like to hear Elijah." You would want me to drop down into a seat pretty quick, and let the old prophet speak. And what does he say? "How long halt ye between two opinions? If God be God, then serve Him; if Baal, then follow him."

He called to a nation that was in need of decision. That is what Chicago wants to-day; for you serve either God or the devil. You cannot serve both. Oh, I believe the curse of the day—the present day—is this worldliness that has come into the church. People try to serve both God and mammon. They are trying it in Chicago. But no man can serve God that way. No. He must have the whole heart. He won't accept of any other service. My friends, it is decision we want. It is not more sermons, not more light, but to obey the light we have. I have come this morning in the hope that I may call you to decide what you will do. I spoke to you of Solomon and Elijah.

I will speak to you of another person you would like to hear. You would like to hear Paul, and I can imagine your saying to yourselves: "Yes; wouldn't I like to hear him. I would walk a hundred miles to hear Paul." If there is any man who is my ideal of a preacher, Paul is that man. Well, suppose him here. What does he say? Behold, to-morrow is the day of salvation? "Behold, now is the day of salvation. Behold, now is the accepted time."

This day, this hour, this moment! I have no right to speak to you about to-morrow. Only three weeks ago I talked long and earnestly with a dear friend, and he has just been followed to his grave; and this morning and last night, at midnight, I thought of different texts; and different subjects came up to me that might stir the church of God; and it seemed to me that I heard it said—so impressed was it on my mind—that there might be some one in the congregation who would never hear a Gospel sermon again. There may be some one here, and he may never hear my voice again; and so I took for my text this matter in hope that there might be some who would hear my voice this morning, and, hearing it, would heed.

Oh! I beseech of you, my friends, don't spurn the gift of God. If I could only picture eternal life, I would have one sermon, and would go to heathen nations and take an interpreter, and just tell it out. But I cannot do it. I have tried many times to describe what it is, but somehow or other it seems that my tongue is tied. If I could but picture what eternal life is, we should see a great rush into the kingdom of God this morning. We would flock into the kingdom by hundreds and thousands, if only we could see what it is; if we could only grasp this tremendous thing—the eternal life of the soul. What is life here? The world is filled with sorrow; filled with disappointment. As I look over the audience I see on every side the emblems of mourning over the victories of the grave; no circle but what has been broken; no fireside without the vacant chair. Before us all dawns the opening grave. In a little while we must lie down in its darkness.

But think of the life where there is no care; where the natural strength never becomes abated; the eye never grows dim; where the pulse is always firm; a city that has no cemetery; where death

...ever comes; where sin never enters—for all that is sweet and pure and lovely is in its native clime. There we should be in the presence of our dear Lord, and our bodies would be fashioned like unto His own glorious body, and we shall be with Him for ever and for ever. Blessed eternal life!

What is here but banishment compared to such eternal life? To go on the Board of Trade and make a few thousand dollars; what is that? To live a few years; what is that? Nothing at all to be mentioned with the life of the redeemed souls stretching in happiness on and on and on, beyond the grave.

And this is my charge: "The wages of sin is death; the gift of God is eternal life." Will you, my friends, have it this morning? Man! will you take it? Come, my friends, will you not tell me you are stretching out for it with every sinew of your soul; and will you not now embrace it to your hearts? Oh! if you will take my advice, you will not go out of this house this morning until you have eternal life.

The last text: That is the promise. The Scripture says: "If thou shalt confess with thy mouth the Lord Jesus, and believe in thy heart that God raised him from the dead, thou shalt be saved, for with the mouth confession is made unto salvation;" for the Scripture says, "Whosoever believes on Him shall not be ashamed."

Now, dear friends, there is the promise—that if we shall confess with the mouth the Lord Jesus and believe on Him, thou shalt not be ashamed.

I believe that a great many are kept out of the kingdom of God because they are ashamed to confess. If they could get into the kingdom of God without the cross, they would be very glad to get in. If they could get into the kingdom of God without confessing, they would be willing to go in. But this taking up of the cross, this self-denial, this it is that keeps thousands out from the kingdom of God. Why is it that Mohammed has got so many more disciples than Christ, many ask me. It is because his follower does not have to deny himself of the lusts of the flesh like the follower of Jesus Christ. I believe that the fear of the cross is keeping hundreds and thousands out of the kingdom of God. But if you want to meet Christ you must meet Him at the cross; and if you want Christ this morning you must take up the cross. What is the cross, I would know. It is different things to different persons.

I remember when last in Edinburgh a business man came to our meeting. He had made up his mind that he ought to live right, and that he ought to have a family altar. And as he hurried his wife and children up the next morning his wife said, "George, what's your hurry?" And he went into the parlor and said: "I have a confession to make this morning, and I want to have you forgive me.

You have never heard me say any words in prayer. I am going to commence this morning. I want you and I want my children to help me." And then he got down and confessed his soul as well as he could. That was the way he took up the cross; and I do not know of a man who was ever more blessed with God than that man. He met God at the cross. Make up your mind that He tells you that to-day is the time; that He tells you to call upon Him now. Will you respond to His call? Will you give yourselves henceforth and forever to Him?

Once, I remember, a lady came into the meeting I was at, and she came in like many others, just out of idle curiosity. She and her father, her brother and her sister had been making a good deal of sport of the meetings; but she thought she would go in. There was not anything in the sermon that seemed to touch her; but there was a lady at her side, and when the meeting was over this lady spoke to her kindly, gently, in winning accents. The lady threw up her head haughtily, and said, "I don't like such kind of preaching." But the other lady asked her to come again, and she came again, and this Christian woman soon won her affection. She came to see this lady, and promised to have a little talk with her, and came back again and again.

But what kept her from the kingdom of God for about a week was that she had to confess before her brother, her father and her sister. She knew what bitter opposition there would be from them. But, she said, if the Lord would take the burden she would take the cross. She went home and told her father that she had made up her mind to become a Christian. The opposition became very bitter. "Now, won't you tell us what you have got there?" they asked her. She answered: "In the first place I have got self-control." And she says: "You know, sister, if you had said half the many unkind things you have said to me since I have been converted before I had been converted, I should have answered back. Then I have got peace, too—peace with God, and peace with all around." The sister broke into a flood of tears and exclaimed, "I have not got them." "Go with me to the meeting," the other answered. They both went and became firm friends of Jesus. But the father was firm in his convictions. He said he would never be known to be at such meetings. He was ashamed of people going to such places. But the sisters worked along together, and finally they told their brother that Mr. Black, of the University, would speak that night. The young man turned pale and said: "There must be something in it; I will go to-night;" and that friend led him into the kingdom of God; and he had only been a Christian six weeks when he died, and he called his father and said: "Was it not a good thing that

Black got up and spoke? Was it not a good thing that I became a Christian?"

Oh! dear friends, you may be spending your last summer, your last winter on earth. Take the cross. Take it up, and thou shalt be confessed to the Lord Jesus. Oh! that you may be saved; that you may be blessed just now. Let us unite in prayer.

EVENING SERVICE.

At the evening services the congregation was fully as large as that in the morning, and there was visible on the vast sea of faces upturned to the earnest speaker on the platform an expression of deep interest and emotion. Occasionally as the voice of the evangelist pealed out the promises of God to those who love Him, and the punishment to be meted out to the wicked, here and there a handkerchief was raised, or a low sob broke upon the ear.

The services were opened with an offering of prayer and song, after which Mr. Moody announced as the text of

THE SERMON.

Mark xii., 34: "Thou art not far from the kingdom of God."

In this chapter, he said, I suppose the Saducees and Pharisees both had met to attack Christ; at least they had come asking Him questions in hopes that they might entangle Him, and get Him to say something that would give them occasion to stone Him to death. After He had silenced them, and they could ask him no more questions, a lawyer asked Him which was the greatest commandment of all. He answered Him, and the lawyer was obliged to say that He had answered well, and Christ made this remark to the young lawyer: "Thou art not far from the kingdom of God." I am afraid if Christ had not made that remark we would have put Him down as a caviler; that He had come in the same spirit that the Saducees and Pharisees had come; but Christ was a prophet; He could read this man's heart; He could see that this man could tell the difference between the external and the internal; that it was not just a matter of form with him; that he knew that the law of God was pure, and that he knew the spiritual meaning of the doctrines that Christ had come to teach. Now, there was no class of people that thought they were so near to the kingdom of God as the Pharisees did; and there was no class of people that were so far from the kingdom of God as these very men. They were the most difficult class of people to teach, and it is so to-day. You can reach the abandoned a great deal better and easier than you can reach the elder brothers and the Pharisees.

Now, suppose that we had been in the temple when the Pharisee and the publican went up to worship, we would have put the Pharisee down as a noble man, already in the kingdom of God, or, if not, very near it; and we would have said that the publican was a good way from it. But God can see more than we can see; the Pharisee was near the kingdom of God, but the publican passed right by and went in. In another place Christ said to the Pharisees, "The publican and harlots shall go into the kingdom of God before you." Why? Because they repented and turned from their sins. The kingdom of God is wide open; the door is wide open to any man that is willing to repent of his sins and turn to God, but the man that is drawing around him the rags of self-righteousness, and thinks that he is better than other people, is a good way from the kingdom of God.

The object of the text and of the sermon to-night is to call your attention to a class of people—I think it is a large class—that come very near the kingdom of God, and yet miss it. I think you will find the world is full of that class of men—that is, their representatives. Cases have been recorded, and I think it may be a warning to us. I never noticed until lately how Herod, who took the life of John the Baptist, was once very near the kingdom of God. If a man had said to me a year ago, or two years ago, "Did you ever think, Mr. Moody, that Herod came near the kingdom of God?" I should have said, "No, I do not think he ever came near it." But there was one passage of Scripture that I had overlooked. Let me read it. It is the sixth chapter of Mark, verse 20: "For Herod feared John, knowing that he was a just man, and heard him gladly."

Now that shows that Herod was brought under the influence of John's preaching. I can imagine when John was preaching there in the wilderness there was a great crowd standing upon the banks of the Jordan, listening to that wonderful man—one of the most wonderful preachers, perhaps, that this world has ever had or ever will have. Most any man can get a crowd in a city, where people throng and are numerous; but it is quite a different thing to get people together off in the desert to hear a man preach. Here was a man coming into the wilderness of Judea without reputation, without fame, without a long title to his name—just a mere voice crying on the banks of the Jordan, and that mighty audience flocked by thousands to hear him. I can imagine, as he stands there preaching the glorious gospel of the kingdom of God, that many who had been looking into the future, trying to catch a glimpse of the coming one, must have been thrilled as he stood there proclaiming the glad tidings; and while he was preaching in that way I can imagine there was a great commotion in the congregation, and, perhaps, if Herod once in a while had heard him—the idea that Herod should go to hear a street preacher—that he should leave the palace and go to the banks of the Jordan to hear this man!

Every eye was upon him. Every once in a while you would see

them looking around to see how Herod took it; and I can imagine they perhaps saw a tear in his eye, because it says he heard him gladly, and not only heard him but he done many things, and if you had gone into Herod's court in those days you would have heard him talking of John the Baptist. I will venture to say there was not hardly one who would talk about John the Baptist but who would be told: "You want to go down and hear that man preach; I never heard a man preach like him; his words come right straight from the heart; I never heard a man talk like him; I never had a man talk to me the way that man did. I have stopped swearing; I used to swear, and I haven't sworn since I heard him preach; in fact I have done a good many things that I would not have done if I hadn't heard him preach; he is just the preacher I like; he talks right at me, and he tells me my faults." He was brought under conviction, and under deep conviction, because when you see a man breaking off this sin and that sin you may know that they have been touched by the spirit of God. And this was Herod; the spirit of God was moving upon his heart; but, alas! Herod made a compromise; he wanted to be a disciple, and yet he didn't want to give up all sin. I believe there are a great many men to-day in the same position that Herod was. I believe Chicago is full of men that have been or are to-night near the kingdom of God; but, alas! they are going to miss the kingdom, because they are not willing to give up all sin; they want to make a compromise. There are many different sins; perhaps he was in the habit of taking bribes up to that time, and he had got to the point where he would not take any bribes. It may be he was in the habit of getting under the influence of liquor and got drunk now and then. He says: "I must stop drinking so much; I must break off many things;" and he was a hopeful subject.

I can imagine after John had preached one day, and then had seen Herod brought under the influence of his preaching, it might have been reported to John, "Well, I do think Herod will be among the inquirers to-morrow when you get through pleading; I think he has almost got to the point, and is just coming to see you after you break up," because John did heal inquirers, you know. Soldiers asked him what they should do; civilians asked him what they should do; publicans, they addressed words to him, and wanted to know what they should do, and undoubtedly many of the disciples thought that Herod would soon be among the inquirers; that he would soon be pressing up to the front to ask John what he must do that he might inherit eternal life. Alas, Herod came near the kingdom of God, but he missed it, and it was not long before he became worse than ever.

Now, I hear people bring this charge against special meetings.

They say they make some people worse; well, there is no doubt about that, but any one that knows anything about the teaching of that book would not talk in that way. The Gospel will be, perhaps, a savor of life unto life, or death unto death. It is the Gospel that softens some hearts, and hardens others. The same sun that strikes upon the ice in one moment, strikes upon the clay and hardens it and the hardening process or the softening process is going on here to-night. Men do not remain the same. You are not the same you were ten years or five years ago. Sermons that would have impressed you five years ago make no impression upon you now. The sermon that would have brought tears to your eyes five years ago would make no impression upon you now, because the hardening process has been going on in that time; men do not remain as they were; men do not stand still; we are going on, either for better or for worse. If some one had said to Herod after he was brought under the influence of John's preaching, "Herod, do you know you are going to take the life of that good man? Do you know you are going to have John beheaded, and do you know you will do it in a few months?" He would have said, "Am I a dog that I should do such a thing? That man with the voice he has? I never heard such a voice; I would rather hear him preach than any man I ever heard in my life. Silence him? I silence him? Never!" Alas! a few months after that and Herod was seven times more a child of hell than ever, and it was Herod that silenced the voice of one of the best preachers this world has ever known; a man of whom it could safely have been said, "Thou art not far from the kingdom of God."

Now let us notice the mistake Herod made; it was that he didn't make clean work of it. No man can get into the kingdom of God that does not make a complete surrender; it is an unconditional surrender that it needed; it is not ninety-nine sins out of a hundred, but it is every one. If a man does not make clean work he cannot get into the kingdom of God. Now there are a good many men want to be saved, but they do not want to give up all their sins. There are some secret sins. I used to think men had intellectual difficulties; there were so many mysteries in the Bible that men would not give their hearts to God, but I have got over that. There is no trouble about getting into the kingdom of God when you are ready to part with sin. Let the wicked forsake his way and the unrighteous man his faults and go to God and be abundantly pardoned. But Herod had a secret sin, his life was not right, but at last John pointed out that sin. Thank God for such preachers. I will tell you, what we want to-day is men who will go into the pulpit and tell you what your sin is. It is not these men who will say "Peace, peace, peace," when there is no peace; it is not these men who will come with oily words and a silvery tongue, men who believe all is right in sin because it is all wrong. The day of retribution is coming. God has got a controversy with sin and is going to punish sin, and if we do not warn men of their sins, why we are not faithful. I am so thankful that John was true, and told Herod that he could not go on sinning; he pointed out his sins. He saw Herod's difficulty; he knew what was keeping him from God; he was living in adultery, and, my friends, I believe the day has come when ministers have got to speak out against this course of sin.

I firmly believe more men and women are kept out of the kingdom on account of adultery to-day than strong drink. A man when he gets drunk goes rolling through the streets and publishes it, and every one finds it out; but this sin is covered up, and it is a delicate thing, and ministers do not like to speak about it on account of the young in the congregation; but the time has come when we have got to speak out, "No adulterer shall enter into the kingdom! No adulterer shall enter into the kingdom of God!" Do you believe it? Do you believe it? Well, if you do, then, dear friends, break with sin, and if that is your besetting sin, may God help you to-night to make clean work of it, and do just as Lot did, flee out of Sodom, turn your back upon it, and cry, "God have mercy upon me. Oh! God, forgive me." I don't know of a quicker way down to death and hell than the way of the harlot, and it is a sin some people seem to make light of; they do not seem to realize it is going to destroy their soul and their body as it did poor Herod's. Yes, he liked John's preaching; he liked his style, he liked his manner, he liked the truth, but, alas, he did not like it enough to bring him out from his sin.

Now, it may be I am speaking to-night to some man or some woman that has been kept out of the kingdom of God on account of this curse of sin. May God deliver you to-night. May that person cry from the depth of his soul, "Oh, my God, have mercy; my God deliver me," and from this night let the cry go up, "Oh, my God, help me; God forgive me;" or your fate will be like that of Herod's.

Ages have passed and Herod—how black his name is! What a bitter end was his! Do you remember after he beheaded John that Jesus came preaching and the news spread through the country, "The crowds are flocking to hear this Galilean." I suppose it was Herod's conscience which rose up. Herod whispered, "It is John risen from the dead." It was his conscience. "John risen from the dead; what will become of me? This man that I have slain to gratify the woman that led me astray; he is living again;" it was his conscience that was troubling him.

But let me pass on, because there are many things I want to call your attention to here to-night. I want to bring to your mind some other Bible characters, and bring home to you your sins in order that you will see yourselves, because that is the object of these Bible characters; it is that we may see ourselves. I believe Pilate was as other men that came near the kingdom of God. He was different from Herod, but he represents another class. I believe that the day Christ was before Pilate was Pilate's golden opportunity; it was Pilate's chance. Every man has his chance, and when Pilate met Christ first, you will remember he was prejudiced against Him; he didn't believe in Him. He believed He was in the wrong, but when he came to talk with Him, he found that he was mistaken, and after making a close examination he came out and said to the Jews, "I find no fault with this man."

He would have been glad to have found some fault in His character; he would have been glad to have found some fault with Him, but after making a thorough examination, this was his testimony: "I find no fault in Him; I will chastise Him and let Him go." What is he going to chastise an innocent man for? Nor do you know the weakness of Pilate's character. Do you know Pilate wanted to be popular? That is all. He wanted to be on the popular side. There is a good many men kept out of the kingdom of God because they haven't got the moral courage to act up to their convictions; they are not far from the kingdom; almost in, but they haven't got the moral courage to "do right and let the heavens fall," if they will; do right because it is right. And when Pilate found out He was an innocent character, he ought to have taken his stand and immortalized himself. His name would have been associated with Joseph of Arimathea, Nicodemus; his name would have been associated with the twelve apostles; his name would have come down through the ages, and shone brighter and brighter as the ages passed away. He would have become immortal if he had only acted up to his conviction; but, alas, he wanted to release Christ and he wanted the applause of the world; he wanted the favor of the Jews; he wanted to hold office a little while longer; poor, vacillating character, and yet how many men there are in this congregation to-night in exactly the condition of Pilate.

You know very well you ought to be a Christian. You know your mother is as godly as the very God you do not serve; you know your early training was true; that it is not now a myth; that it is not now a fiction; but you come up here to Chicago; you have left a praying mother; you have left a praying circle at home, and you have got in perhaps with some skeptic, perhaps with some men who cavil at the Bible because they are living in sin and they want to destroy the Bible in order that they may quiet their conscience;

you know very well if you come out, these very men will begin to laugh at you; they will begin to point the finger of scorn at you and say, "So you are a Christian, are you? You have become pious; you was up to hear that man preach the other night, was you?" "Yes," and yet you have not got the moral courage to stand up like a man and say; "Yes, I have made up my mind I will be a different man." I believe more men are lost because they haven't got the moral courage to say "no" at the right time than for any other reason.

When I was in Edinburgh last winter I heard a good thing. A young man left a praying home and went up to Edinburgh, and he had not been there but a few months before he got in with some fast young men, and one night while they were on their way to a house of shame, walking up Princes street, the great thoroughfare of Edinburgh, the nine o'clock bell struck, and the young man said: "This is the hour my father is taking down the Bible to have family worship; this will be the hour my father will be praying for me," and he came to a halt and said: "Young men, I cannot go with you." "Why not?" "Well, I cannot go with you; I can't go there." Then they began to laugh at him. He says: "You may laugh, but I can't go with you." He turned round; he went to his room and got his Bible down; he got on his knees and cried to his mother's God to have mercy upon him; he found heaven, and to day he is one of the most eminent merchants in the city of Edinburgh, while these young men went down to ruin; they were lost, but this man returned to the fold; he acted upon his conviction. That was the trouble with Pilate, he didn't act upon his convictions. That was his golden opportunity. One step would have taken him into the kingdom of God; one step then and there, and he might have faced Christ and said: "I will die rather than sign your death warrant; you never shall go to the cross; I would rather go there than send you there." It was a golden opportunity, and I say it is a golden opportunity for you to-night to take your stand on the side of Jesus Christ. It is a blessed day; the gates are standing wide open; God invites you to come. Sinners cannot get into the kingdom of God without going to the gate and leaving their sins behind them. Christ is the way, and this man received sinners. The gates of heaven would be closed against sinners, but Christ receives you and makes you meet for the kingdom of God. It is Christ that gets you into the kingdom.

Let me pass on. Here is another case, and that is Judas. I believe there are a great many hypocrites in the church to-day, and I believe that Judas, notwithstanding all he did, I cannot help but believe that many a time he was very near the kingdom of God. I believe that when he sat there on the Mount and heard that wonderful sermon that Christ preached—no man ever heard such a sermon—I cannot help but believe Judas was almost persuaded to give up his hypocrisy and press into the kingdom. I cannot help but believe when he heard him utter those parables that Judas was almost persuaded to give up his hypocrisy.

I believe it could have been safely said, "Judas, thou art not far from the kingdom." When he heard Him or saw Him perform those mighty miracles, when he saw the dead rising out of their graves, when he saw the lepers cleansed and those that he touched made whole, I cannot help but believe that during those three years Judas was almost persuaded to be a real disciple. And I believe there are a good many hypocrites who come to the churches who are almost persuaded to give up their shams and hypocrisy and to come out and be real. And that is what God wants us to do. May God help you to do it to-night. May God grant that this mask may be torn away, and that they may not profess to possess what they do not possess.

It may be that Judas stood near enough to Christ to touch Him when He wept over Jerusalem; and was not his heart touched then? As He came up Mount Olivet to see the city He loved, they were waving palm branches in front of Him, and taking off their garments and casting them in front of Him to do Him homage, but He seemed to forget it all. As He came up that Mount He saw the city His heart loved, and He saw Gethsemane, where He was to sweat drops of blood, but He seemed to forget it all in a few moments. He just wept over the city and said: "Jerusalem! Thou that stonest the prophets; how often would I have gathered thee as a hen gathereth her brood under her wings, but ye would not." Judas saw those tears trickling down the cheeks of the Savior, and do you tell me he was not then and there almost persuaded—that he was not then almost persuaded? There was the King, and he was invited into the kingdom; but, alas! he missed it. And is not that the thing that makes eternity terrible to Judas? I believe it is far worse for him than if he had never heard of the kingdom. It is far worse than if he had never heard the sound of the gospel.

And I pity, from the very bottom of my heart, the man or woman who has attended the faithful ministry and heard the word of God, Sabbath after Sabbath, and has turned a deaf ear to the invitation and rejected the offer of mercy and goes on and dies in their sins.

If I had made up my mind to remain out and not become a Christian, I would never hear another gospel sermon if I could help it—never! I would never allow any man to talk to me about the kingdom of God. I would never read the Bible or any religious book. I believe we will take away with us into another world all the memories of this. You may go out of this meeting to-night and in ten minutes forget all about it; but there is a time coming when God will say;

"Son! daughter! remember!"

All these things will come back, and you will remember every sermon you ever heard. You will remember the text to-night; you will remember how this meeting was brought together this night; how these people looked on the platform, and how they sang these gospel hymns. You will remember how they sang:

> "Jesus, lover of my soul,
> Let me to Thy bosom fly."

And you will remember the text to-night and what I am saying to you. You are not far from the kingdom; some of you were almost persuaded to take the step that would have taken you into the kingdom; but, alas! you did not take it, and it will be worse for you.

We are told many of his disciples went back, and they walked no more with Him. Sad day! They went back; and they walked no more with Him. I suppose those disciples were very near the kingdom—they were almost in the kingdom. One step more would have taken them in, and it could have been said of them:

"Thou art not far from the kingdom."

But some accursed sin, some secret sin kept them. It was going to cost them too much to take up their cross and be laughed at by men, and they went back. But do you tell me that to all eternity they do not regret that step? And is there not an army of such now—almost disciples; almost ready to give up the world; almost in the kingdom? They get so near they look in. One more step would take them in, but, alas, like the children of Israel, when they came up to Kadesh Barnea they laid themselves down in the wilderness, when they might have gone in from Kadesh Barnea into the promised land. I believe that Felix was just in that condition when he said: "Go thy way this time, and when I have a convenient season I will call for thee." I believe he meant to call for him again. He heard the mightiest preacher that ever preached on this earth—Paul. He stood before Felix and he reasoned with him on righteousness and judgment to come; and when he got to that point of judgment to come, perhaps God opened his mind, and it swept on until that day when he should stand before the Judge of the earth and render an account of the things done in the body. Felix trembling said:

"Go thy way this time; not to-night."

Is not that the condition of many here to-night? Am I not speaking to more than 500 young men that are saying: "Wait! Not now. Wait until I go into business for myself. Wait until I am a free man, and then I will attend to this business, but not to-night." Almost like Agrippa, but not altogether. And if you are only almost, I think it is far worse to be almost, and not altogether persuaded. It is a fearful thing to come near the kingdom and miss it.

And now let me ask you a question. Begin here and let the question sweep right up through the gallery, and go to every one in yonder gallery. Has there not been some one time in your life —let your mind travel back into the past— can you not call to mind some one night, or some one hour when you were near the kingdom? The word of God came to your soul with power. It might, perhaps, have been the midnight hour, when you were called to stand by the bedside of some loved member of your family, who was just leaving you. They were launching their frail bark out on the ocean of eternity, and they said:

"Now, I want you to promise me that you will meet me in the kingdom of God."

And the powers of the unseen world seemed to lay hold of you that night, and after they were gone you saw them silent in the arms of death. You went to your room and you said:

"Yes, I must settle this question. I must be a Christian."

Have you never passed through that scene? Have you never passed that station? Come, say, friends, to-night. Just ask yourself that question. Have you not been in a state of mind of that kind?

Or it may be that the spirit of God came in the time of a great revival in the denomination to which your family belonged; that your mother was a member of; and your Christian friends gathered about you and pleaded with you, with tears in their eyes, to become a Christian. That loved mother could not sleep nights, and she spent her days in fasting, and she seemed to travail again over you. She went to God with you in prayer. She said to you:

"If you would only come, my boy, I will be the happiest woman in the world." Or: "O, my daughter! won't you come into the kingdom? I will be so happy if you will only say you will;" but alas! you did not say it. And now you have come to Chicago, and you have got in with free-thinkers and atheists, and you have forgotten that scene. "Thou art near the kingdom." Yes, you were near the kingdom some hour in your life. Some hour the word of God came and knocked at your ear. There was a gentle knock, and you inquired who was there, and a still, small voice whispered, "Jesus. I have come to save you and take you into My kingdom. I have come to take you into My family and make you a joint heir with Myself." And you have been almost persuaded to say, "Yes, Jesus, I will take you; but wait a little: not to-night; not now."

Perhaps five, or ten, or fifteen, or twenty years have passed and you are farther from the kingdom of God to-night than you have been before. The sermons that impressed you ten years before make no impression upon you at all now. You can laugh at death. You can go down and attend to your business and can forget everything you have ever heard about it.

I remember some time ago hearing of an eminent divine, who said it was a solemn thing to see 2,000 persons listening to a sermon on eternal things; but I will tell you something more solemn than that. It is to meet them ten minutes afterward and hear their levity. They have forgotten all about it. Is it not true that many here to-night have been very near the kingdom, but to-night you can laugh at this sermon? You can make light of this text, and you can say without any trouble: "Jesus, go; I don't want you. I have no desire for you. There was a time when I thought something about you, because my mother was such a beautiful Christian. I could see Christ in her face; but she has been gone so long, and those impressions have been all wiped out, and I am a great ways from any serious thoughts." Is not that the condition of many hearts to-night? Now, dear friends, let me to-night plead with you to get into the kingdom of God, let it cost you what it will. If it is thy right eye, out with it. If it is thy right hand, off with it. If it is thy right foot, let it go. It is better to go through life halt; it is better to be maimed; it is better to be blind down to our graves than it is to miss the kingdom of God. I would rather be torn to pieces, limb from limb, and my heart torn out of my body and be with a glorious hope of immortality than to live a hundred years and lose heaven at last. If you miss the kingdom of God it would be far better you had never been born.

Now, are you not near, some of you? Am I not speaking to men and women who are saying to themselves, "I ought to be a Christian; I ought to settle this thing to-night; well, then, I will do it. God be good to me, God helping me, I will, I will!"

Do not be "almost persuaded," but be altogether. I remember of reading, some time ago, of eleven men in the Alps, in 1870, that were coming down through one of the passes, and there came up a sudden snowstorm, and these men got lost, and they wandered around for some time, and at last they dug themselves out a place in the snow, and laid themselves down. The next day guides were sent out to hunt them up, and these eleven men were found within five feet of the path. Five feet more would have taken them into the path, and taken them safely to the hotel, to the inn; but they missed it. They might as well have been five hundred miles from the path as five feet. There they were. They came near saving their lives, but they missed it. And so, dear friends, to-night are you not near the kingdom? Is not God in our midst to-night? Don't you feel the working of the spirit of God? Is it all imagination? Is this all a myth, a fiction? Is not the spirit of God brooding over this audience to-night? I have no more doubt that the spirit of God is trying to woo you to Christ now, than that I stand before you. There have been a good many prayers gone up to God to-night for this meeting. You have the power to spurn and reject his offered mercy. Now, what will you do? You have the power to say, "Go your way," or you have the power to receive Him. What will you do? Will you step into the kingdom? I once heard a man get up and say, "There are three steps to heaven." I thought that was a very short way. Only three steps; out of self into Christ, out of Christ into glory. But there is but one step into the kingdom; out of self into Christ, and that is glory. Just one step takes you right into the kingdom. The door is wide open. God wants you to pass in to-night. Dear friends, there is no power on earth can save you against your will. I imagine some of you saying, "Why don't God save me against my will?" I can only say, He don't. He don't want machines in heaven; He wants sons; He wants to draw you by the cords of love. He could save you against your wills, but He don't.

Let me ask you this question: He gives you Christ, what more can He do? If you are waiting for God to do something more toward your salvation, what more can He do? Just think a moment. I believe a great many are kept out of the kingdom of God because they think God could do more toward their salvation. But I tell you God can literally do no more than He has done. He has sent us prophets, and we killed them; He has sent us his only begotten Son, and we took him to Calvary and put Him to death. We know when a man goes into a court and the court decides against him, he takes an appeal and carries it to a higher court, but here men decided that Christ should go into the grave, and the angels took Him to a higher court, and God took up the appeal and put Him upon the throne. Now, what more would you ask Him to do for your salvation? Can He literally do any more? Dear friends, God has done all that He can do. Now, you accept what He has done. Do not leave this house until this question is settled. I think some of us would be willing to spend this night here if we could only have the joy of knowing that we would enter the kingdom of God. I think I would be willing to stay here until the sun gets up to-morrow morning if God would give us some hope; if you will say, "We will not leave until we have settled this question." Let the decision come to-night. Say to-night, "I will go into the kingdom of God if I can get in," and you will soon get in.

Now, I can imagine Satan, while I am preaching, is at work with you, saying, "Don't be carried away by that man; don't you act rashly; be calm; be quiet; don't you do anything on the impulse of the moment; plenty of time; take your time." Now, bear in mind that is the devil's work. Do you think the Lord Jesus would whisper to you and say, "Don't you decide to-night." Would your godly praying mother say to you, "My son, don't you decide this to-night; don't you be in haste about it; take your time?" Do you think your mother would do that? Have you got a true friend on earth that would ask you to put this off to-night? Not one.

Now, dear friends, I do not want to leave this pulpit to-night without warning you that procrastination is the greatest enemy the human race has got. If Satan can get you to leave this church to-night without deciding, he has accomplished his work; for to-morrow there will be a hundred things that will keep you from deciding this question. Far better at the close of this holy Sabbath evening take your stand and press into the kingdom of God. A few years ago, on the Old Colony Road from New York to Boston, just before the train came up, a farmer saw near his house a land-slide. There was not time for him to get to the railway station and telegraph the night express to stop it, and he did not know what to do. He took his lantern and went up the track, and just before the train came he fell down and broke his lantern. He could not get another, but he was terribly in earnest, and he took the broken lantern and hurled it at the engineer. The engineer mistrusted something was wrong, and he whistled down brakes, and the train was stopped within a few feet of the land-slide. I throw a broken lantern at your feet; dear friends, take warning. Before I come back to Chicago again many of you will be gone. Will you die inside the kingdom of God. Will you die with the glorious hope of immortality? May God keep you from missing heaven. Let us unite in prayer.

The congregation bowed their heads, and Mr. Moody offered the following prayer:

Oh Lord, bless the words that have been spoken to-night in weakness. May they be carried home and bear fruit, and may old and young to-night press into the kingdom of God. Oh, that our hearts may be rejoiced to-night by seeing hundreds give their hearts to Thee. Oh, that angels may rejoice in heaven over the souls that shall be saved here. We praise Thee for what Thou didst do this morning. We thank Thee that Thou wast with us, and oh, this night may hundreds be saved. Oh God of Pentecost, give us a Pentecost this night, and may there come a wave of blessing over this congregation, and now at the silent hour, at the close of this solemn meeting, may the still, small voice be heard throughout this building. May there be many that shall hear the gentle voice of Jesus saying: 'Come unto me all ye that labor and are heavy laden and I will give you rest.' Let the weary find rest here to-night. May those that have been cast down for months and years, may they cast their burdens on Christ just now, and may there come sweet peace and rest to their weary souls. Oh, Son of God, pass this way to-night. Go through this congregation, and while we are praying and the silent prayers are going up from many, may the dew of heaven come upon the congregation and may the powers of the world to come fall upon us just now. Make this place awfully solemn. May we hear Thy voice, and now, while the voice of man is hushed, may the voice of God be heard.

Speak, Lord, to every heart, and to every conscience. May the deaf hear Thy voice and may the blind to-night see Christ as they never have seen Him before. Oh, God, do this for Thy Sonship, and now while we are waiting on Thee silently, wilt Thou speak, and may many hear Thee saying, "Behold, I stand at the door and knock; if any man hear my voice and open the door I will go in to him, and sup with him and he with me." Jesus, Master, come unto all our hearts. Oh, we invite Thee to come, and may the proud heart to-night yield. Help us to unlock the door. Help us to unbolt it. Help us to open it and give Thee a royal welcome. Oh, blessed Master, just now deliver the captive. Help these men to give up their besetting sin. Help these men to turn to right from every sin and to be wholly Thine; and may there be an influence go forth from this meeting that shall make glad the city of our God. Amen.

At the close of the services in the main hall a meeting of seekers after the truth was held in the lecture room, and a large number placed themselves in the ranks of the army of the Lord."

FIRST DAY OF THE CONVENTION.

The excellent report of the proceedings of this memorable convention, furnished daily by "The Inter-Ocean," was fitly prefaced by the following remarks about Farwell Hall and the accessories of the occasion:

THE OPENING.

Nature seemed to sanction the good work inaugurated yesterday morning in the fair opening of the Christian Convention. It was veritably a "day of joy and gladness" beneath the bright sky; it was all this and far more within the walls of Farwell Hall, where, at 9:30 o'clock, there had gathered between 2,000 and 3,000 Christian workers from far and near, with ears to hear and anxious, docile hearts to believe. At 9 o'clock they had begun to throng the large hall, that was to be taxed to its utmost capacity. Phrases from the Scriptures, intoning the spirit of the hour and the convention, were displayed about the edge of the gallery. They read, "Love the Brotherhood," "God Is Love," "Pray Without Ceasing," "Behold how good and pleasant it is for brethren to dwell together in unity," "Rejoice evermore," "Your body is the temple of the Holy Ghost," "That they all may be one as Thou, Father, art in me and I in Thee, that they also may be one in us, that the world may believe that Thou hast sent me."

Upon the high wall back of the platform was hung an enormous chart that is well intended to uplift its mute appeal in behalf of foreign missions. It depicts by means of squares, each representing a million of people, the actual and relative numbers of mankind, according to their religion. Its showing of the prodigious discrepancy existing between the number of the souls of Christendom and heathendom can but prove a standing text for each humble worker of the convention whose influence, however slight, goes for good in the slow and laborious process of universal Christianization. The chart shows the world's population to be divided as to their religion and want of religion as follows: Protestants, 116,000,000; Greek Church, 8,000,000; Roman Catholics, 190,000,000; Jews, 8,000,000; Mohammedans, 170,000,000; heathens, 856,000,000.

After the opening exercises of prayer and singing, the subject and the first speaker were announced by Mr. Moody, namely:

Rev. Dr. E. P. Goodwin, pastor of First Congregational Church, Chicago.

"HOW CAN WE BEST SECURE A PREPARATION FOR CHRIST'S WORK."

Speaking to this, Dr. Goodwin, with that power that has secured him a conspicuous eminence in the Congregational pulpit, said: Dear friends, you could not possibly be more disappointed than I am that it should have been appointed to me to have a word to say here instead of the brother whose name is upon the programme. At a late hour last night, after an exhausting day's work, including a trip to Graceland and work on missions, I was told that this brother might be absent this morning, and I would be expected to take his place, but still when I came here five minutes ago, I hoped that some other arrangement might have been made to relieve me. But I should be sorry not to respond to my duty to do all that I can do, especially after so long an absence from the city, and after so great gladness has been put into my heart on my return by seeing such a work commenced already as this one proposed by this convention; not waiting till the mid-winter, but going forward thus early, as if the Lord's people would say—how shall we best, in these beautiful autumn days, put ourselves in training for doing this great work and for deserving great blessings. It seems to me that the Scripture way of putting the matter is about this: That God is always prepared, and that there is nothing we need to see to, excepting that the people prepare themselves the right way for the doing of the work.

You find many a passage in the Old Testament about preparing the way of the army; nothing about the Lord. But the people have sometimes a good deal to do about getting ready. And chiefly of that it might be said, as the brother said, that the first thing to do is to get the hindrances out of the way, to prepare the way of the Lord, by gathering up the stones, as in the old time when preparations were made for the king's coming—the highways swept smooth, the stones gathered up, and everything put in readiness that the great monarch could come without delay. You will notice this thought in the Bible. Let my first suggestion or first thought, then, be this: The way the Lord will have His people prepared for His work is, first of all, to get a view of Him. You will notice in the 6th chapter of Isaiah where one of the Lord's servants, in preparing for a special work and message looking between God and people, the first thing prominent is that Isaiah is not found in a convention nor in a circle of even two or three, but personally He is alone with God. Dear friends, it seems primarily necessary for you and me as workers to bear in mind that the first fundamental condition of our success and power is that we shall go alone with God. These are the days in which God is thought little of. These are the days in which God is made little of, in which God is largely cast out of the thoughts and minds of men.

These are the days of such pressure of business and absorption in worldly matters that men either at home or in the study find little time for communion with God. I am sure I speak the mind of ministers, of brethren, when I say that it is one of the hard things of this day to be alone with God; and I am sure we shall fail in our work unless we get before us the proper conception of who God is; that before all else, over all business, over all pleasures, over all home life, over all other sources that impress us, the great conception that is to inspire us, the great fact that is to rule us is that we are God's people, God's ministers; seeking first of all how we may glorify Him. You will find that among all the long list of prophets who had any special work of revelation, that somehow in the very earliest stages of it, the prophet is closeted with Him, like Abraham, like Gideon when the angel of the Lord comes to him; like Elijah. Look at all the prophets. When in the work to which they were called, they were with God. It was sometimes a month, not merely an hour. It was a closeting with God, like that of Moses where he bows down on his face until the forty days and forty nights are accomplished. Great things come from praying; from finding out God, from being with God, from seeing God, from feeling as God feels.

And the only conception, it seems to me, we can get from their examples is the consciousness that in us dwelleth no good thing; that we need cleansing and purifying. The first conception of the prophet is that I am unclean, and he thought that because he had been with God, he must needs perish; but lo! there was cleansing, and he was purged from his sins, and he could go out and declare his message to the people.

Now, brethren, I am sure for myself, for you, that in this first hour, the first thing, the supreme conviction of our hearts is that God is here, and the dearest wish of our hearts is that we may know God; that we may be like God; that we may be filled with the power of God; then we shall be put in the way of being so; we shall have made the best preparation, and, I think, the best way traced out for doing work; work that shall glorify God in these coming days. Then will come what our brother has referred to. You remember in the Scriptures, God's people are spoken of as vessels, as the old vessels of the temple, down even to the very smelters and the articles of the least significance, although sacred as used in the service of God.

You will find that when, in Nehemiah's day, they held great gatherings, perhaps like these, they read for hours every day the book of the law. You will discover all their names written to the solemn covenant to God that they would keep His law, obey his commandments, cleanse themselves from every form of defilement, and from that time be His people and His alone. I am sure there is meaning in that. I am sure that if we are willing to have God's spirit poured upon us we shall be willing to cast aside our pleasures and pride of the flesh. I am sure if we are willing to do that, to put all things of the home life and the business life temporarily aside, and write over all, this is for the glory of God; to take, every man his lips, his hands, and his feet into the closet, and say, as the old priest said, these shall be kept for God, these are for the service of God—we shall have for ourselves solved the question that will get its blessing of answer, for every quality, and in every home, in every business place, the power of God; and the power of God will not longer tarry to come upon us for the salvation of souls."

Mr. Moody, a man who never lets the anvil forget the ring and touch of the hammer, or the white heat of the ductile iron dissipate itself and nothing shaped, briskly rose and said, "Major Whittle will follow on this question." Thus introduced, this home evangelist, who has made his campaigns against Satan, and Southron as well, addressed the audience in his firm, tuneful, and measured way.

Major Whittle presented three questions which should be answered. The first was personal experience of what conversion to Christ was. The second was to study God's word, and the third was to have faith in the presence and power in the spirit of God.

The speaker, in reference to the first question, read from Paul's Epistles, giving the personal experience of the great apostle. We were to lift up Christ as a personal Savior, to be witnesses to what we had seen and heard and no more. We could not be witnesses to anything more than we experienced personally, and that was all that was expected. It was no credit to a man to be converted, and it was no discredit not to be converted. There might be, there were, many persons in the churches who had not had this personal experience that they might stand as witnesses to a personal Savior.

They had never been brought to a personal knowledge, but were standing on the forms of religion. The speaker had known of ministers who had not had this personal experience, and they failed to exert that converting power that was necessary to the work. This personal experience was the preparation we needed. We were to search our hearts, to drive out forms and find a personal Savior. Then we would find ourselves prepared to do Christ's work.

In the Gospel of John we were commanded to search the Scrip-

LIBRARY
OF THE
UNIVERSITY OF ILLINOIS

tures. There were three things for which we should search the Scriptures—for history and biography, for moral truth, and for spiritual power. Martin Luther studied his Bible on his knees for years before he was used by the Lord. John Knox studied the Scriptures before he was called to do any work for the Lord. So it was with all men. They could not expect to be useful servants and called to do important work for Christ until they had studied the Scriptures that they might find what was His work.

We were to be filled with the spirit. If we, standing on redemption ground, preached the word, that preaching would have the power to convert. We were given the promise of success. God was just as anxious to fulfill His promise to-day as He was at the Pentecost.

Prayer was offered by the Rev. Dr. Herrick Johnson and hymn 93 was announced, Mr. Moody requesting that it be sung softly, for all should remember it to be a prayer. So in a prayerful key the invocations were uttered, "More holiness give me, more strivings within." The opportunity for five-minute talks on the foregoing topic was then given by Mr. Moody. H. L. A. Stevenson of Boston, by the aid of illustration and anecdote, showed that the secret of a hallowed life is found in personal communion with God. The growth and fruitfulness of a tree depended upon its unseen root, unless the tree were a Christmas tree, which bore its crop all outside. The Christian lives of some men were like the fruitage of Christmas trees—hung upon the outside.

"Oh! happy day," was then started by Mr. Sankey, and the obedient voices of the many hundreds took up the glad refrain.

Mr. Moody concluded the discussion with one of his plain talks, striking home in every sentence. He said: I once heard a man say he had a very good well with two exceptions. It would go dry in summer and freeze up in winter. There were a good many Christians like that well. They are good in spots. What we want is an even temperature, good for 365 days in the year. It is this spasmodic Christianity that is doing so much against our work to-day. They are enthusiastic for a time and then they fall back into the cold.

There must be a personal experience and an evenness. One way to secure this is to call together all the hungry in our churches. There may not be a dozen in any one church, but let them come together, for it is often in such small meetings that we find the richest results. We are told that "Blessed are they that do hunger and thirst for righteousness, for they shall be filled." When I came home from England in May last I found that an old oak tree near my house was still filled with the dead leaves of last year. I tried to pull the dead leaves off, but I found that would be a big work which I could not hope to complete soon. One bright morning I found the leaves nearly all off, and the new buds were putting out, showing signs of the new life. This new life, new sap, was casting off the old life. There are a good many old things in our lives that should be cast off by the new life. Let us pray for this blessing. Let us pray for this new life. Let the motive, however, be pure.

Too often our motives are not right. We want to take up the service before we receive the holy life. This is not right. We want the holy life first. Paul never said anything about winning souls, and is it not strange? No. He was enthusiastic for Christ. He spoke always of knowing Christ, and when we come to know Christ we may then take up His service and win souls.

There are three ways of knowing persons. We know them by hearsay; we know them historically. Another class we know by introduction, but we don't know much about them. We have heard their names, but that is all we know. Then there are people that we know intimately and have known them for years. There are men on this platform that I have known for twenty years, and it seems to me I learn something more of them each day that I live. There are three ways of knowing Christ.

Some people know Him historically, just as they know Napoleon and Cæsar. They know Him from what they have heard of Him. These people come into the church because they think it a duty, or it may advance them socially or in their business. There are others who know Christ slightly. They talk and talk, but don't say anything. They are as sounding brass. Their talk don't amount to anything. There are too many in the church who have no testimony to give. You can count on your fingers those who can give personal testimony for Christ. They are like Lot in Sodom. He was for many years there, and said to be an influential man, but when it came to the test it was shown that in all those years this man had not converted one soul. He even lost part of his family in that great destruction. There are paying members in the churches, but they are not praying members. The result is that the church has little power for Christ.

The woman at the well was taken into immediate service by Christ, because she could give personal testimony, and we see that she went out and at once turned the town upside down almost. If we run into the field without the Master we will fail. That is the reason we see so many failures among those that are working for God.

There followed a few moments of silent prayer, and afterwards the audible petitions of two of the brethren upon the platform. Again the worship of song was resumed in the quartet singing of

Messrs. Sankey and McGranahan, Mrs. McGranahan, and Mrs. Carrington, the congregation participating in rendering two of the stanzas.

The hour—eleven o'clock—for the consideration of the second topic, "What are the great hindrances to Christ's kingdom, and how can they be removed?" had arrived, and the Rev. Dr. J. H. Barrows, pastor of the First Presbyterian Church, Chicago, allotted twenty minutes for his subject, was introduced.

"THE GREAT HINDRANCES."

Rev. Dr. J. H. Barrows prefaced his remarks by saying that others would point out how the hindrances were to be removed, his duty being to show what they were. This pulpit orator, whose speech rung as virgin metal, proclaiming clear, true thoughts, bred 'mid the refinements of a generous scholarship, advanced to the front to hold his audience, saying:

This question, as it stands, is world wide, nay, wide as the universe, for we have scriptural authority for believing that some of the obstacles and enemies of the Christian Church are extra-mundane. Paul wrote to the Ephesians that they were wrestling with fallen angels of different orders, that they were struggling against wicked spirits in high places.

Here are obstacles or foes that we cannot remove, and to guard ourselves against which the Apostle urges to take on the whole armor of God, girdle, breast-plate, shoes, shield, helmet, and sword.

If we consider merely the hindrances which are earthly and sensual, omitting those which are devilish, we are brought face to face with a variety of obstructions, and different observers, occupying different points of view, will vary in their judgments as to which are the most formidable. The Rev. Dr. Jessup, of Syria, looks on Mohammedanism, reaching from the hearts of Africa to the heart of India; Mohammedanism, with its iron cruelty and hardness of spirit, blasting the lands it controls, and blinding the minds that inherit its faith as the chief obstacle to the Redeemer's kingdom. The English missionary, toiling amid the 260,000,000 of India, regards the frightful system of caste, with its immemorial grip on Hindoo life from the cradle to the grave—caste which is rooted in an abominable theology, and in its essence is the contradiction of the spirit of Christianity, as the one mighty barrier to the regeneration of the most populous of the continents. The Christian worker in Japan looks on that empire as the key to the redemption of Asia, and finds his chief enemy in the skeptical, materialistic philosophy which the emancipated Japanese mind is rapidly imbibing from the translations of Renan, Strauss, Spencer, John Stuart Mill, Paine and Ingersoll. The American missionary in France, Austria, Spain, and Italy regards the downfall of Romanism, with its false doctrines, its corrupt practices, and its persecuting tyranny, as the one thing needful to the speedy triumph of the gospel.

Joseph Cook returns from a tour of observation around the globe, and finds the chief obstacle to the progress of Christianization in what he calls the "semi-universalism" of the home churches, paralyzing missionary enterprise. Many a Christian pastor in America or England reading of $700,000,000 wasted annually in strong drink in each of these lands, a larger sum than the church has expended in foreign mission work for 300 years, noting the demoralization which drunkenness produces in the great centers of population, seeing its alliance with all that corrupts and degrades our political and social life, many such a pastor has come to regard intemperance as the one prodigious hindrance, the one heaven-defying obstacle to the kingdom of righteousness, purity, and good will. If I should put to you the question which I am to discuss I should get a great variety of answers. Some of you would find the main hindrance to the rapid advance of our Redeemer's kingdom in the weakness of the pulpit, in the decline of Sabbath observance, in the selfish extravagance of church members, in the wastefulness of the use of tobacco, in the lack of that parental consecration which devoted the children to God's service, in the unwillingness of Christians to do personal work for others, in the church's comparative neglect of the great masses of our city populations, in the dread of revivals, in the lack of thorough Bible study, and so on. And doubtless every answer thus far given has truth in it, though the truth may not be one which it would greatly profit this convention to consider.

What we need to perceive clearly and feel deeply is not so much the external hindrances as those that are within the church.

I once asked a little company of earnest Christian workers what was the most frequent excuse given by impenitent persons for not coming to Christ, and they unanimously replied: "The faults of Christians." And if we take an historical survey of Christianity we must be convinced that opposition from without has been weaker than corruption within, that Hophni and Phineas rioting in the tabernacle had dishonored the Lord and defeated His hosts more than the Philistines fighting for the ark. Reading the history of the church, our distress and shame are not so much over the attacks of cruelty and unbelief as are the lapses of false teachers of the truth, priests turning practical atheists, right conduct disregarded in the attempt to secure church conformity, worldliness and sensualism creeping in among the successors of the apostolic fishermen, and of Him who had not where to lay His head, wranglings among the friends of truth, the church lowering its claims to please secular power or to capture the worldly, Cæsar consummating a diabolical marriage with the Lamb's wife.

In those times when the church has been cold and sluggish and self-centered and oppressive, the weapons of infidelity have been forged. I have recently read a remarkable book called "Underground Russia," written by a Nihilist, who describes the fearful revolutionary world that plots and dares and dies beneath the throne of the Czar. He narrates the story of the attack which infidel socialism has made on Russian institutions.

The first onset was on Christianity, and this, he says, was the easiest citadel to capture. Translations of the leading works of German and English unbelief were scattered over the empire, and Christianity, as a system of national belief, was destroyed in the minds of all cultivated people. In a land where such things could be done, the Christian church must be in a sink of imbecility and immorality. Allied with a tyrannical government, disgraced by the lives of corrupt priests, feeding the people on the pictures of saints and not the word of God, the Russian church had no practical arguments wherewith to meet its foe. The triumphs of unbelief to-day spring from precisely the same causes with the triumphs of the heathen over the children of Israel in the Arabian desert, and in the promised land, the disobedience and faithlessness of God's own people.

In times of special religious interest, our sins, our shortcomings, our imperfect lives rise up, a mountain of offense, between many men and salvation. They look on us rather than Christ. It is a deplorable fact that when men's minds are turned toward the Lord Jesus, they are sometimes turned away by the sight or knowledge of our moral delinquencies. They argue that if Christianity does not make men more upright in business, more trustworthy in their promises, more generous, gentle, humane, and courteous, then the gospel is a practical failure.

I know that God's grace gets hold occasionally of some crooked sticks, and they always show thereafter something of their natural bent. "Grace," it has been said, "is like lightning; when it strikes a man it follows the grain."

A coarse-fibred man may be converted to God and yet need a vast deal of pounding on the anvil of God's discipline. An intensely selfish man may become a Christian and always be more distinguished for prudence than for generosity. A mean, crafty, unscrupulous man, like Jacob, may be converted to God and require a semi-annual reconversion before he is fitted for companionship with the Apostle John. There is need of a vast deal of charity for men who inherit terrible constitutional obliquities or violent passions that come down through a long series of ungodly generations. And we must also remember that God does not perfect human character immediately. But looking on Christian men generally and on the average, they may rightfully be expected to exhibit a conspicuously higher morality than others. It is not enough for us to say that when men make comparisons they choose a poor specimen of a Christian, and the best specimen of an unbeliever. It should become plain to all the world that the church aims directly, continuously, and with all earnestness to make men truer, juster, purer, more helpful, and more loving in every human relationship. We must show that we believe not only in the Christ who died on Calvary the atonement for sin, but also in the Christ who, as the teacher of righteousness, proclaimed the sermon on the mount.

But the main hindrances to the cause of Christ are not the flaring sins which bring reproach on the Christian church. The sin of Ananias and Sapphira, the sin of Peter in denying his Lord, the sin of Judas in betraying his master, these exceptional transgressions which you can put your finger right on and puncture with righteous indignation are not those which most grievously dishonor Christ. The body of Christ has received many wounds of this sort which have been quickly healed.

Worse than a wound is general debility, a languid, low-toned vitality such as people complain of in the spring of the year, when they sigh for Peruvian bark and tonic bitter drinks. Malaria in the church atmosphere, breathing depression and inertness over the great body of believers, is often worse than swift and terrible disease striking down a few. When the cares of this world have choked the word into unfruitfulness, when a systematic avarice fills up the routine of lives externally honorable, when luxurious worldliness has usurped the place of a self-denying other worldliness of mind, then it is that we cause the name of Christ to be blasphemed, then it is that the sound of the Spirit is dulled, then it is that the heavenly flame is most completely smothered. A Christian woman has described God's work of redemption as a fire. As soon as it was kindled men tried to stamp it out, but it spread all the faster. Then they tried to drown the fire in rivers of blood, but the fire rose up through the blood in brighter splendor. Then the engulfing waters, heathenism and skepticism, rolled over the fire but the flame was not quenched. At last there came a snowstorm, millions on millions of little cottony flakes, falling, falling, falling, day after day, week after week, year after year, on the divine fire, and it almost went out. The dreadful quenching storm is the cold indifference, the manifold worldly cares, the delicate dropping innumerable snowflakes of earthly interest and distraction, which more than outward persecution and unbelief have subdued the fire of the Holy Ghost.

A spiritual, pure, self-denying, consecrated church, united with

Christ in His death to sin, united to Christ in the new and risen life of holiness, united to Christ in separation from the world, united to Christ in toil and suffering and blessed expectation is God's mightiest force among men. It was for such a church that Jesus died, that the spirit was given, that the New Testament was delivered to men. It was for this that God's saints have suffered persecution and martyrdom. It was for this that in times of corruption God has raised up John the Baptists and Martin Luthers. A pure and Christly Church. Before such a church unbelief will be stripped of half its armory of strength. By such a church the forces that attack heathenism will be augmented ten-fold. Vital interests of benevolence will not appeal in vain for adequate support. The great evils of the land will be checked, for the church will sever the chains which have bound her to much that was iniquitous and more that was questionable.

Two things ought right here to be considered. One is a fact of history, the other is a fact of revelation. The historical fact is this: that the external hindrances were never so great as at the beginning. The mountains that confronted the feeble, hated, and despised church in Judea overtop the hills which lie before the church of to-day, with its powerful hand on the civilization, the riches, the science, the commerce, and the learning of the leading nationalities of the world. Our internal dangers may be greater than those of the infant church that felt the tide of love

"Stream on her from her Lord's yet recent grave,"

but no such vast, complex, malignant, and mighty external forces are now linked in unholy and seemingly invincible alliance against the gospel as at the beginning.

The fact of revelation is this: Omnipotence is our ally. Back of the day of Pentecost was a divine command to evangelize the nations. Back of this command was a colossal "therefore." Back of this "therefore" was the declaration of Him whose hand built the heavens, and had laid that hand on the cross from love to the world, and had smitten the might of death, and was about to ascend to the throne of infinite majesty. "All power is given unto me in heaven and earth." "Go ye, therefore, and teach all nations, and, lo, I am with you always, even to the end of the world."

If the church then is at any time weak and fearful, and cries out as did Judah before Ammon and Moab, "We have no weight against this great company," it needs to hear what the spirit of the Lord said through Jahziel, "The battle is not yours but God's." During the great struggle in the British Parliament over West India emancipation, Sir Thomas Fowell Buxton kept his Bible open every day at the fifteenth verse of the twentieth chapter of Second Chronicles. And it would be well for the church daily to read, "Be not afraid nor discouraged by reason of this great multitude, for the battle is not yours, but God's."

Therefore, it seems indisputable that one of the chief hindrances to a more rapid spread of the gospel is our failure to see our Divine Leader as John saw Him—on the white horse, with bow and crown, going forth conquering and to conquer. The secret of the church's power is not in glittering ceremonials, or vast machineries, or prosperous organizations drawing the fashionable crowds, though I believe thoroughly in Christian ceremonies, and Christian machinery, and in endeavoring to bring the rich to Christ and to His church.

The secret of Christian power is the alliance of our souls by faith with the loving heart of Him who called Abraham from a life among idolaters to a life of trust in Jehovah; of Him who empowered Moses to carry the burden of his people's woes because he lived as seeing the invisible God, of Him who gave victory to Joshua and to all who in human weakness have leaned confidently on divine strength. There is a doctrine of divine sovereignty which has made heroes, men of high enterprise and valorous achievement, which has armed the sling of David with might above Saul's or Goliath's spear, which made Elijah victorious over Ahab, which gave to Paul and Luther and Whitfield a spiritual power that has moved the nations. We deplore the unspirituality of the church. What do we mean by it? Partly this—that Christian disciples have, like the unbelieving world, fallen into distrust of spiritual forces. They believe in many things, in works of charity, in intellectual preaching, in boards of benevolence, in a hundred excellent things, but they do not heartily and practically believe that the church is supported and made efficient by supernatural power, they do not believe in the Bible doctrine of prayer, and this is resolvable into unbelief in an ever-present and almighty Lord, sovereign, gracious, and available to all the needs of his church. Dr. Fairbairn relates in a recent work the story of "a sturdy Scot, valiant in speech as in deed," who as English Embassador to the Court of Prussia sat at the table of Frederick the Great, then meditating a war whose sinews were to be mainly formed of English subsidies. Round the table sat French wits of the infidel sort, and they and the king made merry over decadent superstitions and the follies of the ancient faith. Suddenly the talk changed to war and war's alarms.

Said the long-silent Scot: "England would, by the help of God, stand by Prussia." "Ah!" said the infidel Frederick, "I did not know that you had an ally by that name," and the infidel wits smirked applause. "So please your majesty," was the quick retort, "He is the only ally to whom we do not send subsidies." The outspoken faith of the sturdy Scot in the alliance of Jehovah with Christian England illustrates the living faith in the all-sufficiency of Christ, which is the secret of the astonishing power which is sometimes wielded by the church, a faith which needs to be quickened in many of our hearts. One remark only, in closing, as to the method of removing these hindrances. It is a method which aims at a thorough and widespread revival—a revival from within the churches, not a general movement which sweeps along outside the great mass of our members—but one which, beginning, it may be, with the pastor's own heart, reaches into all our Christian homes. Such a revival, coming from the Holy Spirit, through a simpler and more direct preaching of Christ, and in answer to faithful and persistent prayer, will sweep away the miserable obstructions to a glorious spiritual life in many of our churches, will send forth multitudes to preach the gospel in the streets of Chicago and the streets of Asia, will cause new and abundant riches to flow through the channels of benevolence, will answer a thousand cavils of unbelief, and be a stream that shall gladden the city of our God.

At the conclusion of Dr. Barrows' address the congregation sang, "My Faith Looks Up to Thee," followed by Mr. and Mrs. McGranahan, who sweetly rendered "Showers of Blessing." Prayer was then offered by Bishop Fallows, and the second speaker, by appointment, on the question treated by Dr. Barrows was introduced.

Rev. C. L. Goodell, pastor of Cong'l church, St. Louis, Mo., continued the discussion, and in a simple, direct way, forcibly set forth some of the hindrances to Christ's kingdom, indicating at the same time how they might be removed. All the hindrances, he said, were on the side of Christian people. These hindrances were cruel things, obstacles in God's highway, and should be hated. As torpedoes were placed in the way of the Czar of Russia, which, exploding, killed him, so modern infidelity was planting torpedoes and waiting to see them explode, and the church thus overthrown.

The first hindrance was a want of honor for God's house and respect for His ordinances. While he loved the home, there must not be forgotten His love for the gates of Zion. His house was dishonored, and yet how easy for all to put such a hindrance away, and the house of God be filled. How great the blessing that would fall when the old sentiment of loyalty to God was again turned.

A second hindrance was the tendency to show and display in worship rather than one to open the fountains for the thirsty that they might come and drink. If there were to be cast out of God's house all that did not tend to edify and save men, how much would go; but there would be souls left to take the water and bread of life unto a new service. Stitching on this and that beautiful apparatus would not save men. Let the word sweet and pure be given them, and instead of losing the house and the people there will be a gain, for where the water is there will the thirsty come.

Another practical hindrance, perhaps raised unconsciously, was the seeking to gain hearers rather than doers, multitudes rather than converts. It was one line of policy to fill pews and make things grand so that how many will say, "We've got the right man now; this one will convert the world." But there was a line of work which tells over this mere hankering for numbers; it was that in which one sought to convert to Christ, and shape the life of the church around Christ, seeking to bless and to save men. Heaven sent forth such a man and the power was given him to lead others.

Another hindrance to be removed was the resisting of the spirit and the grieving of the spirit of God. This was constantly done by all, for man loved the world and resisted the call. The power of the church went out, but there was no arrow to the mark.

Another hindrance was the loss of the first love. The mightiest in the home is the love of husband and wife for each other. They love each other, and will sit by each other through the year, bearing burdens for each other. Love was strong. It was the strongest thing in the church. It was the unity of the church. The love of Christ in the early church made it mightier than Cæsar. It carried it through deserts and over mountains.

What we want in this city is to go back to our first loves, and let all our being go out to Christ. Another thing is faith. The word was pronounced often. We wanted a practical, earnest belief in what Christ said. The faith men were the mighty men. The skeptical men were weak, and they had never accomplished anything in this world. It was faith that helped Columbus to find out this new world. No skeptic would ever have accomplished what that faith man accomplished. The disciples were not able to cast out evil spirits, because of their unbelief, Christ said. It was the same unbelief that was weakening the church to-day. We needed more faith. We needed to believe as the church believed when it went out to conquer the world. Faith would conquer, and did the church have faith it would conquer. Prayer and faith and love and righteousness were the powerful things in the world. When we had these we need not fear the sinful things.

Dr. Goodell had hardly finished when the leader, Mr. Moody, was on his feet and talking a race with the seconds, as though he was trying to make a ten-minutes' speech in the two minutes left of the morning session. "One great hindrance," said he, "is so much talk about the hindrances. The less said about hindrances the better. [Laughter.] I have known a great many congregations to be discouraged by talk on the dark side. When a man loses heart and

LIBRARY
OF THE
UNIVERSITY OF ILLINOIS

D. L. MOODY.

becomes discouraged, he begins to look on the dark side and is not fit for God's service. You can't find from Genesis to Revelation where God has ever used a discouraged man. Four times he tells Joshua to take courage. The moment that he gets his eye off from God he begins to look at the darkness and the walls of Jericho, and he says, "We are not able to go up and possess the land." But the Lamb is going to prevail. It has become a lion. Let infidels talk as they will, Christ is going to prevail. I heard a man in Boston talking about the wickedness—just as you people have been talking about the wickedness in Chicago. Don't talk about the wickedness. You can't convert it by that. I said to my Boston friend who was so discouraged, "Have you any doubt about the final result?" He looked at me a moment and then said, "No." He had never thought of that.

Well, Christ is going to triumph. Let us not talk about discouragement then. Let a minister go into a church and talk that way and he will carry his discouragement into all the pews. Why, don't you remember, it is promised that one shall chase a thousand and two shall put ten thousand to flight. It won't take long to put all our enemies to flight in that way. When a child is linked to God and heaven he is a power. You remember what a power old Elijah was on Mount Carmel. He was more powerful than Ahab and all his court. They were not to be compared with this one righteous man. But the moment the old man got his eye off from God he was weak as other men. When he kept to his text he was strong, but when Queen Jezebel sent to him her threatening message he began to think of it instead of God and went over and sat under a juniper tree to grieve. There are a great many Christians sitting under the juniper trees like the old prophet. What we want is courage and hope. Let us look on the bright side. Let us remember that it was a succession of victories from the manger to the the cross. The men of that day, however, thought it was a failure. They thought it was all dark when they laid away the Lamb in the tomb, but on the third day they saw Him rise a lion. Let every one of us remember this, and that Christ is bound to triumph. Let us look on the bright side."

With hymn 118, by the congregation, the morning session was concluded.

THE NOON MEETING.

But who thought of leaving? Few, indeed. The hour for the noon prayer-meeting had arrived, and the announcement was duly made by Mr. Moody. He bade the people move into what seats were vacated, and hymn 334 to be sung. There really seemed no decrease in attendance. During the entire morning there had been men standing in the rear of the auditorium, and both gentlemen and ladies had hunted out some "coigne of vantage" on the gallery stairs leading to what may be called the proscenium. So the prayer-meeting became a continuation, in the matter of close attention and interest, of the morning session proper. After the hymn prayer was offered by J. W. Deane, the evangelist, and another hymn sung. Then Mr. Moody addressed the people on a theme befitting the designated character of the hour. He called the attention of his hearers to Christ as an example in prayer, a man of prayer. In everything He did He prayed. Again, His prayers were very short. The only one of any length was John xvii. Christ spent one whole night in prayer before the choosing of the twelve, and before that memorable sermon on the Mount. He had heard directly from the Father in prayer. Why might not man expect an answer from Him?

Illustrative of the efficacy of prayer, Mr. Moody drew from the experience of himself and Mr. Sankey, and told with increasing feeling of the efforts of the two evangelists when first they appeared at Cambridge University, England, and set themselves the crucial work of addressing the students, with a view to their conversion. It was a Saturday eve in November, Guy Fawkes night. The first attempt was cruelly discouraging. The students not only applauded the hymn, but the prayer, turning the whole service into ridicule. So it was on the following Monday night. Wednesday the evangelists assembled some of the mothers of the town, and there was prayer. Wednesday night came, and the university meeting was again held. Under the circumstances, and beneath such criticism as they were enduring, Mr. Moody could preach with but little fervor, though he felt that the prayer would be answered. And he asked if there was one young man in the university who had the moral courage to rise and go to the gallery, where he might be talked with by the evangelist. It was an awful test, said Mr. Moody, but at last one arose, and it seemed as if fifty more followed. From that hour until they left, the evangelists found more work than they could do.

A few days ago, in the way of fruits of this first trial, Messrs. Moody and Sankey were asked to return to Cambridge, where they now have the pleasure of heroes in knowing that the good they did lived after them. And what was the agency in all this? Not, said Mr. Moody, in his own preaching, nor in the singing of Sankey, but in prayer. So, concluded Mr. Moody, what was wanted was to get into living communion with God in prayer. Let men get together and see how quick the blessing comes.

When Mr. Moody had concluded, Mr. Sankey announced hymn 356, "All-seeing, gracious Lord," and the congregation joined in with a hearty good will. Prayers were offered by various members of the congregation, when, the doxology being sung and the benediction pronounced, the immense gathering filed slowly down, occupying the sidewalks for blocks in every direction.

AFTERNOON SESSION.

In the afternoon the hall began to fill up an hour before the opening and even before all were out from the noon prayer meeting.

Mr. Sankey came in at 2:15, and went at once to the organ, inviting the people to pass the fifteen minutes remaining before the opening in singing familiar hymns.

At 2:30 sharp Mr. Moody stepped upon the platform, and at once opened the convention by announcing the hymn, "I will sing of my Redeemer."

The Rev. Flavel Bascom made the opening prayer, after which the congregation, led by Mr. Sankey, sung, "Lo! the day of God is breaking."

Mr. Moody said that Dr. Goodell had a church of 850 members and he understood that the pastor knew each one of these personally. He would like to ask how he did this. He understood that the Doctor visited all his people, and he would like to ask how he found time to do it.

Dr. Goodell answered that he made it.

"How do you make it?" asked Mr. Moody.

"I take the time from other things. I spend all my evenings in visiting and do not spend one at home with my good wife. I try to see some one."

"How many members had you when you took the church?"

"I had ninety-two."

"How many have you now?"

"Nine hundred and fifty," was the answer.

Mr. Moody said there was nothing like success, and those pastors who were successful he would like to have them tell this meeting how they succeeded.

He then called upon the Rev. Mr. Weston, of Peoria, to tell how he managed his church.

Mr. Weston said Mr. Moody was a good man to ask questions, and a better one to answer them. He then said we wanted the preaching of doctrine and of duty. Preach that this was a lost world, that the people were perishing on the right and on the left. God had ordained that this world should be saved, but He would save it only through human instrumentality. They should preach to the laymen. God had ordained that all the members of the church army should take part in this work. There were none so rich or so cultured that they had no responsibility in this matter. There were none so poor and so obscure that they were not responsible. All were responsible, and all were to take part in the work. They were to preach this to the people, and not settle down on a few prominent members to do all the work.

When the walls of Jerusalem were to be rebuilt, every one took part and built that portion of the wall opposite his own door. It was not enough though to preach this, but the minister must set the example. The people needed leaders, and the pastors were the best ones to lead.

It was not enough to tell how to do the work, but to lead in the work. If the pastor was going to take strongholds of sin, he should ask his people to follow him.

Then there must be organization if the church was going to do anything. The hit or miss style would not do. Every one working as he pleased might do in some cases, but it was by systematic work, thorough organization, that the work always could be depended upon. The church people were surprised at the success of the politicians who were able to move the whole country. It was because the politicians were organized, and when they struck a key note the whole people heard. God's people must be as wise as the world's people, and then they would be as successful. In organizing church works there must be a place made for every man, and every man fitted to a place in which he could work. Let each class work where best fitted.

In his church Mr. Weston said he had four classes. He had the little boys of the church work in one department, the young ladies in another, the young men in another, and the married ladies in the fourth.

Dr. Goodwin asked Mr. Weston what proportion of his church he succeeded in bringing into the work by this plan.

Mr. Weston answered that the proportion varied with different times in the year, but on an average he believed he had fully one-half at work. At certain seasons, as now, the opening of the year, when they were preparing the winter's work, the proportion was somewhat larger. But he did not always use the same plan in getting his people to work. One plan would do for one year and the next year they would need an entirely different plan. He changed his plan of work every year.

It was asked what Mr. Weston did with his married men. He answered that the majority of the men of his church were railroad men, and they had to work day and night, Sundays included He could not very well put them into harness. But they worked in the young men's class. He had 800 members, and had built it up from a small mission.

Mr. Moody here took up the discussion.

He spoke of a gentleman in New York who had been inquiring

about Mr. Weston's church. A man in New York had died and left about $1,250,000 for this good friend to invest where it would do the most good for Christianity. He was looking out for the good places.

This was the most vital question that would come before the convention. They wanted practical men and women in the churches. They did not want any sleeping members. In England silent partners were called sleeping partners. There were a good many people who had an idea that the Lord wanted sleeping partners.

In London there was a church called the Church of Ease. A good many people thought the churches were all places of ease. They were not. We had an eternity in which to rest. We should work while here. We needed leaders. It was said that Cæsar's success was in saying "come" instead of "go."

Mr. Moody had twelve propositions to lay down.

First, let the church lay out its work.

The second field of labor was to let those who were competent go into the Sabbath School.

The third was to secure for leaders in church work those who were leaders in society.

Fourth—They should get all the music possible into the church, and get all the singers into the choir. Let them sing the best they could; do not quarrel with them if that is not very good. Mr. Moody said he could not sing much, but when he sang the best he could that was as much as Mr. Sankey could do. Singing was a great power in the church. The Methodists had sung the gospel clear round the world in a few years. They should get the lay element to work and get them to sing. Get five hundred in the choir if that many wanted to sing, for their preacher would have a good congregation in the choir if no place else. Let all join who wished. If they did not sing in time let them sing the best they could, and get them to sing from the heart. Mr. Moody did not know anything about time, but he could tell when people sung from the heart. With good music the preachers would preach better. About one out of twenty in the churches were fond of fine music, but the other nineteen were not, and he would advise that the one be allowed to look out for himself, while the churches looked after the nineteen.

He told a story of two doctors, one of whom was better in his studies, but the other was more successful in practice. The student wanted to know the reason for the other's success, and he replied that only one in twenty people stopped to think. The student was after the one, the other got the nineteen. One went for class, and the other got the patients. The preacher should not be always looking after the cultured, the educated, the people of influence. Let him look after the people.

Fifth—The non-church goers should be looked after. There should be a record kept of such people in the parishes. Have them visited often, and after awhile they would go to church to get rid of the visitors. The idea that we should open the churches and invite the people to come was not the idea of the Gospel. That was to go out and bring the people in. We were to be seekers. Mr. Moody would have a committee to visit the non-church goers. The minister should look to it and have people in the church who did not want strangers in their pews, fill them up with their friends. The pews should be full, and if the pew-holders did not fill them, let the ushers do it.

He then told several incidents showing how church people often drove strangers from their churches by coldness and a lack of interest in them.

There should be a committee to visit the sick. It was folly to talk about the minister being the best person to visit the sick. The speaker said he would rather go almost any place than to a sick room. He never had been sick in his life, except sea-sick, and he did not know how to sympathize with sick people. He wanted those who knew what sickness was to do this work, for none would know better how to express sympathy and give comfort. He would also have a mothers' committee. Not one minister in one hundred could talk to young mothers and give them advice. The ministers could not rear their own children. To talk to the young mothers he wanted the godly mothers who had reared families. We wanted to make these young mothers practical. He would also have a committee of the best and pleasantest people in the church to meet strangers when they went to the service, and show them the best pews.

Mr. Spurgeon gave up the best pews in his tabernacle to strangers, and for that reason his church was popular and he had a great field. We should not think too little of other men's talents, and think they could not do anything. Every man could do something. Every one had a talent for something.

He told the story of a Swede who could not speak English who asked to be set to work in the meetings held in Farwell Hall several years ago. Mr. Moody had not known what to do with the man, but at last sent him out on the corner of Clark and Madison streets to give out bills. The man had a sweet face and it was always beaming with smiles. He could not understand English and he staid there giving to every man that passed a bill. Sometimes a passer-by would curse him, but the poor Swede did not know but it was a "God bless you," and sounded sweeter than ever.

In Edinburgh the ladies of the churches went down into the poor district and took charge of the babies of the mothers there while they came to his services.

If there was any class of people he sympathized with it was these mothers with large families, deprived from all outside comforts. He hoped the time would come when mothers would be invited to bring their babies to church.

This proposition seemed to be understood by a little one in the rear of the hall, for it set up a cry that would have discouraged any speaker but Moody.

The audience laughed at the incident. Mr. Moody was not in the least disconcerted, but said:

I like to hear babies cry. One of the best things I ever saw was a big, strapping fellow trying to lull a crying baby to sleep while its mother was in the inquiry-room. The babe had been crying and the mother was almost distracted. The young man watched her for awhile and then said: "You go into the inquiry-room and let me take care of the baby." And he took the child in his arms while 8,000 people looked on and strode up and down the aisle with it while it cried. If they do cry it won't drive me from the pulpit, nor do I want it to drive the mothers from the meeting. If the child cries aloud I can speak louder.

Mr. Moody lifted his voice a pitch higher, while the baby in the rear of the hall, which had continued to cry, raised its little voice until it was almost a match for that of the speaker, and the audience again laughed. Mr. Moody, proceeding, said he was preaching in London once when a ferryman came to the meeting, who was allowed to do so by one of the wealthy men of the church running the ferry during his absence. Another way to interest the people was to invite the church-goers to call upon the non-church goers. It would benefit both.

The topic of the afternoon was:

"HOW TO INTEREST THE LAY ELEMENT OF OUR CHURCHES."

The discussion was opened by the Rev. C. L. Goodell, D. D., of St. Louis, with the following address:

The purpose of this convention seems to be not to discuss new truths, but practical truths; to stir the movements of old creeds in Zion, that they may bring forth old churches to better service. Truths are very simple, and yet to handle them so as to bring practical results requires great skill and devotion of heart and spirituality of life. To pick up the doctrines that we have heard and apply and connect them so as to make it better is no slight thing. God only can help us to do it; and the application of these truths and principles, that seem so commonplace because we have heard them so much, is the question we have before us.

How to set to work the lay elements in our church is a very practical and important question. It may be divided into two sections. First, the doctrines that incite to effort; second, the methods by which it is to be directed.

To consider first the doctrines that incite to effort. In a cold, dead time in the Church of England, when the hearts of people were spiritually dead, in the diocese of Winchester, a powerful preacher was set to stir the clergy. From all over the diocese they came together to hear him. He announced his subject as "The existence of God." "Why," they said, "that will not quicken our hearts. I supposed he had brought to us some new truths, some truths that would startle us." But the outcome of the service was this; he said: "If God does exist, His threatenings are true, His promises are true, and anything revealed concerning Him is true, and they are burning truths. We must prepare to meet our God in all our shortcomings. Prepare now to meet thy God."

The sermon broke up the spiritual lethargy of his hearers, and they went to their homes and worked powerfully. That sermon sent them home to work, sent every man into his vineyard with his spade. Now, so must we do as ministers and Christian workers to-day. If we would set the people to work, speak of the Lord Jesus, speak of His wondrous love, of His great sacrifices, of His saving cross, of His righteousness, of His truth. Preach Christ. There is no truth under heaven so fit to stir the heart; there is no truth so fit to interest a true man, year after year. Nothing is better than to listen to the preaching of Christ from the uplifting on the cross to the wonderful story of His love. The old, old story! It will stir the heart to service.

It will inspire all the finest qualities of the heart to work. So the minister who wants to draw the people to work and stir the soil in the vineyard and make every tree fruitful—let him begin with Christ; let him preach Christ and Him crucified until all the people see the cloven side and grasp the bruised head. The person loving Him the most will do the most in His vineyard. The person whose soul is most faithfully imprinted with the worth of His sacrifice, is the person who will be best, in and out of season, in drawing souls to His feet. And the minister and worker who keeps nearest to him will bring others nearest to Him. And the man who does most in leading will do the same for himself. How essential is it that we preach the word baptized in the blood of the cross; vitalized and made pure by the Holy Spirit.

A thousand things may be preached full of novelty and attraction; but soon they go out, and leave the whole a desert. But he who preaches Christ and Him alone, and sets forth the words of redemption, is the one who will succeed. His work will be hallowed by the Lord. Now we have tried to do this. We have sought to preach Christ, and to set forth His truth. But we must be near Him at first. We must be warm in his doctrine of grace and love and mercy. We spoke this morning of the hindrances to the spirit of the kingdom of God.

In every heart is the want of grace. Christ's words on tender and melting souls melt under the power of Christ's love. For that person who seeks that power every hindrance is overcome, and there is no obstacle to that believer. He sees Christ. He sees the power of God and the wisdom of God unto salvation to every one that believes in Him. Now, it is the preaching of great truths that makes great preachers. This it is that makes great men; great churches, powerful churches. This it is that makes institutions; that places great eras in Christian history.

What brought the Puritans to plant the Word of God in this country? What brought them here but to unite together in worshipping God? What has taken missionaries around the globe, carrying the cross far and near? It is the shining cross in their own hearts. Having tasted Christ's love they carry it to others; having known His salvation themselves, they are anxious to deliver the message of redemption around the globe. Now nothing but this will accomplish this great thing. Men are not sent as ministers to please the public. The church is not a cow to be milked for them. They will not get any cream if they do. They are not sheep to be shorn of their wool. If they try it they will only get bristles. It is not more respectable to preach the gospel than to plant corn. It is not that. That style of Christian worker never will move the Christian world. It must be Christ's great doctrine of salvation, the truths as they are in Him, that must be preached. And a man to be powerful must be nearer to Christ than his hearers if he would lead his church nearer to him.

A celebrated divine of England said to be otherwise was like a man meeting another on the side of a mountain; both were the same height from its top and its base. But the one was going down to the base out of the light, out of the wide-spreading glories of the sun, out of the glory of God, to the shades below. To turn him was no promise of success in power. The other man, though level with him at first, was passing to the summit, when God spoke, when God's word was revealed; passing to the summit, caring nothing for suffering, caring only for spiritual power to save souls, because he had the heart that loved Christ's kingdom. It is going in that succeeds, not coming out. The word blesses more and more it is sought, and draws nearer and nearer our hearts to God. It quickens all the community. These essentials are of exceedingly great importance.

If we want power with which to fill the church, keeping out no man, a great procession marching along God's highway in truth and praise, we must be filled with Him and speak for Him, and live in Him. Now this is the doctrine.

If a man preach this, and teach this, and live this—there are the elements of the mighty church, of a powerful, spiritual community. Such truths beget sons and daughters of God. Such truths quicken and vitalize society. Such doctrines build up, and never pull down, and where the word of God is so given out with the believing heart, a heart trusting in God, and beating with the love of God, there will be blessing indeed. There will be movement. It will be the stream of life.

The church will be the river of God, and as it flows on it will be separated according to the various conditions of all. Here into prayer sunrise, here into Sunday school work; in other places according to the ability and fitness of the people.

Then comes the question how to utilize this power that this truth has awakened, that such doctrines have begotten, that such fullness and presence of Jesus in the church has inspired? How, I say, shall we utilize this power, and quicken and gather the saved up, because the soul that is not set to serve soon perisheth; loses its energy; wastes its power. When Saul was converted he asked, "Lord, what wilt Thou have me to do?" This is the question of every soul when converted.

What will the Lord have me to do? When Christ ascended to heaven, His disciples stood around the Mount of Olives, and in a little time Christ sent an angel down to stir them up—an angel straight from His throne to put them to work. Then came the Pentecost and the fire; then the zeal everywhere working—founding churches. So the faithful pastor, the true preacher, the successful Christian leader, will be careful to take all this fire and intelligence and love and devotion, and turn off into channels of usefulness and high Christian endeavor. Now what profits it if you melt the one in a furnace and do not draw it off, but simply go again the next day and melt it, and again do not draw it off, but let it cool in the furnace? And yet how much just such work is done like this. Men go to prayer-meeting and associate together and rejoice. They do not go next day to see a sick brother, to look up a wandering Sunday-school scholar; do not go to work among their own children, but simply continue in the old way until next meeting, and then heat the ore over again. This is barrenness. The ore is soon burnt and spoiled. The pastor should be a wise master-builder. You must send out the runner, the swift of foot, throughout the parish, throughout the community, as a flame of fire that will send hearts that have been kindled, to your church; to your Sunday services and your week night services.

How do you get water to the family across the way? The

water will never leap from the river to the house. Men must lay the pipe. How is a room in a house to be lit? A pipe must be laid from the gas-meter to every room in the house you want lighted. How are we to bring this Gospel of Christ to those who do not go to the meeting when the fire is kindled? By making every person take a live coal and touching with it the lips of the other brethren, of the child and brother who go wandering, of the lost soul. In my early parish there was opposite my study a beautiful little home. A fountain played before it; a wide lawn encircled it; shady trees protected it, and a lovely household filled it. Day after day I prayed to God earnestly that His Spirit might come to them, and that they might be saved. One day, standing there watching the house—God had not yet answered my prayer, but time was going on—they seemed as far from the water of life as ever. Standing there I saw the gas burning in a rooms of the house. It had been "brought" there. Water played in the fountain. It had been brought there by patient effort. God spoke to me in that thought. I asked myself, "How will Christ be brought to them unless you are the conductor? Go to them." And that afternoon I went to the house. Soon the lady bowed in prayer in the parlor, and gave her heart to the cross. Soon her husband was led to the Lord, and the whole family. That was the greatest lesson that has ever come to me during my ministry. I said afterward that I would lead the living stream to perishing souls; and I venture to say that a thousand souls have been redeemed to the cross through the providence of Christ.

And I give the incident to-day as a practical way in which we are to take Christ to others. When I asked the lady if she would accept Christ, she said, "I will. I have been hoping you would come around and see me many a day." How many in our parishes are waiting for the word! How many are waiting for the water of life! How many are waiting for the light of life, and we can carry it if we will. Now, there are a few departments of special work—dependencies on the house of God—that the pastor should watch with great care and prayerfulness and spiritual wisdom. I wish to speak of the utilizing of some of the special classes of people in a church, and I commend the words that I have spoken to those that shall hear. The remarks that I shall make will seem to some commonplace. But their carrying out is that which fills the church and keeps the spiritual fire burning on the altars of God.

First, of all; keep the services of the Lord's day open; keep them warm; keep them full of the love of Christ and the power of God. Keep your light lighted. Teach your family to honor the house, the Lord, and the day; teach them that that is the place in which to honor God and in which to expect to receive His special blessing. That old truth made new by the presence of the Holy Spirit will fill our church; give effectiveness to our Sabbath services; produce changes over the entire face of society.

And the prayer meetings and the mid-week services, they have a work to carry on of joy and sweetness, to elevate the world. Let the excellence of Carmel come there, and the sweetness and majesty of Lebanon, so that men shall delight to go to them. Let the Sunday school life be fresh and vital. Let there be an eye on every class, watchfulness and care everywhere. Let there be Bibles and libraries, and maps and other helps, quickening in every way the efficiency and advice. Do not expect that this work will take care of itself.

Then let there be a missionary spirit; let there be a missionary library, for the most vitalized Christian life is beyond the seas, in foreign fields. The home work may have been dimmed for a while, but information shows that it was never more powerful than now in foreign fields. Christianity here feels its influence. It is under its influence, and the work for it, that new light is spreading over it. Let the history of heroic missionaries speak for it; of great devotion; praise it. Let the histories of this work be put into the hands of every child, and the maps of it too. Let the spiritual work be done from house to house.

Let the parish be mapped out and districted, and from all these departments have reports made to the pastor and to each other in meetings.

Let there be cottage meetings in the distant districts, in the neighborhoods where it is not so easy to preach in. Let every week be held cottage evening meetings. Those who first slyly attend these will soon become warm and blessed and become regular attendants upon the larger meetings. Prayer and work, doctrine and duty, truth and light from God carried in the heart along every highway and byway, into every home, and those that are distant and cold shall be warmed, and the parish shall be alive, and God shall be over all, and over the parish there shall be new births into the kingdom of Heaven.

"HOW FAITH SPREADS."

The next topic for discussion was assigned to the able hands of the Rev. S. J. McPherson, of the Second Presbyterian Church, of this city.

"How Faith Spreads" is plainly told in the last words of Jesus Christ, recorded by Luke. He there instructs His disciples that "repentance and remission of sins should be preached in His name unto all the nations, beginning from Jerusalem. Ye are witnesses of these things. And behold, I send forth the promise of My Father upon you; but tarry ye in the city, until ye be clothed with power from on high."

Here are at least three fundamental facts. 1. The power by which Christian faith spreads is "power from on high"—the Holy Spirit—operating through Christ's regenerated disciples. 2. The process of spreading it is by gradual radiation from the vital center of personal faith to the world lying dead in unbelief, "from Jerusalem"—from Chicago—"unto all the nations." 3. The means by which it is spread is the Christianized contagion of personal influence. That is, before we preach the gospel we must possess the power; and our immediate work must always be with those who are next to us; and after we have ourselves become photographic negatives of the living Christ, we must, under the gospel's own light, imprint His image upon men by actual contact with them. As illustrative of this principle, notice a few New Testament symbols—Faith is a leaven. Beginning always in a leavened center, it sends infectious power throughout a lifeless mass by touching every particle of it until the whole is leavened. Faith is a mustard seed. Within it there is found, latent, the force which slowly produces the mustard tree, "the greatest among herbs." Its seed is in itself, absorbing into its energies the inert elements adjacent; it mightily assimilates them to its own nature.

Faith is living water which, rising out of Christ, its original fountain, not only slakes eternally the thirst of every receiver, but becomes in each a new fountain springing up to everlasting life for others. Faith makes Christians the salt of the earth and the light of the world, because they both possess Christ-like character and exert Christ-like influence. Salt preserves; light creates. Salt acts from within, by permeation, from atom to atom, seasoning and conserving whatever it touches; light acts by diffusion, from a center, by radiation, illuminating and quickening whatever it falls upon. Salt is opposed to false profession; light to useless possession. Salt, so long as it retains its saltness, is forced by its natural pungency to preserve; and light is so compelled by its natural radiance to shine that you cannot destroy its rays without destroying itself. For light consists in shining. Faith is a baptism of fire. Burning first in Jesus, and then in His followers, it sweeps outward in all directions; not by leaping over long intervals, but inch by inch, each bit of glowing heart-fuel communicating it to the next; yet it ever burns with the divine energy of the kindling spark. Again, faith is a life. It must reproduce itself. No lower force can generate it. But it will be propagated in proportion to the energy existing in its original source and to the sympathy of those who transmit it.

Faith, then, does not come by chance. It is Jesus Christ reproducing Himself in us and through us, accomplishing at every step the nearest and most natural effect of His power, and instantly converting each effect into a new cause. It is after this fashion that faith has spread in every period of sacred history. For example, when God would obtain a peculiar people among an apostate world, He called not a race, but one man. To Abraham was the stupendous promise given that in him should all the families of the earth be blessed. That promise first awakened Abraham's own faith and made him the personal friend of God; then through Abraham it reached Sarah and Isaac and the patriarchal household. Thence through Isaac and Jacob it descended to the growing race of Hebrews, and thence through Jesus to mankind—the individual, the family, the nation, the world. These are the stages in the propagation of Old Testament faith. The same fact appears in the earthly career of Jesus. He did not send faith down out of heaven; He brought it; He exemplified it; He died for it. Most of His ministry was private, opening the fountain of rapturous faith in a few at the beginning of the stream of Christian history.

For thirty years He illustrated the new life in the strange silence and solitude of Nazareth. Even in his brief public ministry it was rather the exception than the rule for Him to present his gospel to promiscuous assemblies, as when he fed the 5,000, or preached on the mount to multitudes, or made His triumphal entry into Jerusalem. The universal proclamation was rather reserved for a later stage of development; his personal ministry was mainly to "the lost sheep of the house of Israel." He proceeded from the few to the many only so rapidly as he could vitalize those nearest to Him. Hence, He revealed His divine power at the wedding in Cana, to the obscure mourners in Nain, to one depraved woman at the well of Samaria, among the dear household of Bethany, in the wilderness, by the wayside, and most of all among that select school of disciples who were to graduate as His apostles. These he trained precept upon precept, line upon line, making sure that they experienced the grace which they were to preach, and then, after they had become eye-witnesses to the marvelous events culminating in His resurrection and ear-witnesses to the gospel revelations embodied in His own person, and, most of all, heart-witnesses to the regenerating powers summed up in the gift of the Holy Ghost. He sent them forth to communicate to others the divine contagion which they had caught from Himself.

In planting and training the Christian Church, His apostles continued to follow the same method. Pentecost was the original mustard seed, which has grown into the wide-spreading tree of Christendom.

The risen Savior's handful of witnesses, because they were filled with the Holy Spirit, began to speak with other tongues as the spirit gave them utterance, and "the same day there were added unto them about 3,000 souls." One touch of the quickened body of Christ's followers began to waken a dead world to life, and "every nation under heaven" felt the resistless impulse of divine life. From that vitalized center the vital leaven of Christ's grace was steadily propagated in all directions, from atom to atom of mankind's huge mass, until this leaven of the spirit was neutralized in the Roman Empire by the poison of political power, and the life of faith was smothered in the papacy by the smoke of ritualistic incense and of grinding ecclesiastical machinery. Faith declined because the gospel was preached by worldliness and ceremonialism instead of consecrated personal influence. The church became bloated and moribund; immorality honeycombed her with "indulgences;" the "dark ages" ensued. Not until the emancipated monk of Erfurt lifted his face to Jesus Christ, saying "Thou art my righteousness but I am Thy sin," did faith again begin to spread among mankind.

That one man, Luther, transformed by simple faith, became the quick center of the new world of Protestantism. Like Wesley, and Edwards, and Finney, and many others great and small, in our own day, he illustrated afresh the true centrifugal force of Christianity. That is, it spreads by the sole power of the Holy Spirit; it spreads outward from a vitalized heart to dependent extremities; and it spreads gradually, step by step, by a law of personal contact. Without stopping to inquire why the Master has preferred to propagate faith by what we may call this natural method rather than by a perpetual series of miracles, observe how it does in fact spread, now in concentric circles throughout all the spheres of Christian life. Beginning with the outermost ring, it operates thus:

1. In the foreign mission work, whose flourishing periods have always followed times of special consecration in the church at home. For example, it was characteristic of the second stage of apostolic history, when Paul and his colleagues carried the gospel over the Roman Empire. In the middle ages it languished because the church was stagnant at home. To-day it again sweeps over the world in ever-widening waves, because our churches are recovering apostolic faith and zeal.

2. It operates similarly in home mission work. Plymouth Rock, like the stone that smote the image in Nebuchadnezzar's dream, has become a great mountain and is filling the nation. But Plymouth Rock lay dead, the inert plaything of restless sea waves for ages, until it was made a living stone by Puritan faith and prayer. So to-day, in proportion as the Church of Christ in great centers of population is aflame, like the consuming, unconsumed burning bush, do we see the fire of the gospel glowing in the towns of the frontier.

3. Faith spreads similarly around every local church. A church's spiritual influence is in direct ratio to its own faith and fidelity. It can win its neighborhood to Christ, not merely by its wealth, or its culture, or its social position, but solely as these and other talents are inspired by vivid faith in Christ crucified. That Master says: "I, if I be lifted up, will draw all men unto me."

4. But these principles must operate specially in the individual Christian. Indeed, every general movement of faith has been radically nothing more than an aggregate of personal influences. The Church, the body of Christ, is a corpse until it is filled with His spirit, and that spirit acts chiefly through persons. It is not so much by means as by instruments, not so much by humanly organized conventions as by their divinely awakened men, that faith in Christ spreads. Like begets like. The Christian bears fruit after his kind. The believer propagates belief. The duplicate of Christ multiplies Christ among men. "Ye are my witnesses," says the ascending Savior. As for us Christians, Christ is Christianity; so for the world, in a high sense, we are Christianity. The only way, therefore, to spread Christianity is by being genuine Christians ourselves, and then we can hardly help spreading it according to our talents. It is, of course, true that in order to be safe, in order to be happy, in order to have peace with God and with the universe, in order to acquire perfect character, like that of Christ we must be Christian.

But, further than that, we must likewise be completely Christian, in order to be completely useful. As a labor-saving device in the work of doing good, as a matter of mere skill in power to help and redeem mankind, eager faith in Jesus Christ is the supreme thing. The best policy is always the best principle, and the best principle is regeneration by God's spirit. How do we Christian workers long to reach the highest efficiency in Christ's service! Yet it is, fundamentally, but a question of the deepest consecration. O, for the gift to our lean hearts and barren lives of that faith in Christ by which to educate the ignorant for eternity, of the love of Christ to win the wayward back to God, of the power of the living Christ to save the lost, of the self-sacrificing, of the dying Christ to raise the dead to immortal life. Faith will spread by me when it is no longer I that live, but Christ that liveth in me. Let me, then, have at least the beatitude of gospel hunger and thirst.

THE QUESTION DRAWER.

The last half hour of the afternoon session was devoted to the question drawer. While several hymns were sung, the question box was passed through the audience, and any who pleased were allowed to ask any question about practical work, but Mr. Moody said no questions upon controverted or doctrinal points would be recognized.

The first question the evangelist took from the box was as to whether he would preach the law or only the love of God. He said: "The law has its place. I preach more law than I did a few years ago. If a man preaches only one side of the Gospel he will not have success. A man wants to know that he is sick before he want a doctor. He wants to know that he is a sinner before hee will look for the Savior."

The next question asked was: "What would you do if a person were in one of your meetings and should give a shout?"

"I should let them shout once or twice anyway, especially in a union meeting. I have known a great many good meetings to be broken up by a few people who thought they could not be happy without a great deal of noise. Where there is too much wind there is not much thought or work."

"What would you do if you were in a church where the best members would say that they were overworked in obtaining food for their families, and could not work for the Lord?"

"I have never been in such a place. Such men you will find are not practical. They have no system. I will venture that such men waste an hour or two every day. If they will husband their time they can save many hours to devote to the Lord's work."

"Do you think that the evangelist should belong to some church?"

"I do. That is perhaps a hit at me. I do belong to a church, and I was kept out of it for a year because I was not converted. I had too hard a time getting into the church to leave it. I am still a member of a Chicago church, I believe. I never heard of my being turned out. It is the only organization I care to belong to. I have no sympathy with the men who stand outside and try to tear down the church. It is easy to tear down. We want to build up."

"What can be done to reach the non-church-goers?"

"We had that question pretty fully discussed this afternoon. Every man and woman has his or her work. When we work together the world will be reached. But in this country we are fast drifting like the old country. In England, in the manufacturing cities, it is said that 98 per cent. of the population never go to the house of God. Dr. Dale, of Birmingham, thinks this is exaggerted. He puts it at 95 per cent. But even if it be only 90 per cent. it is very bad. These men gather in their shops on Sunday, or some place else, and talk communism or infidelity. They are not poor, for they earn from £3 to £8 a week. They are hard-hearted and hard-headed men, and the men who uphold the cross in their midst have a hard time. We are drifting in the same way in this country. The church should take steps to reach these people. We need a band of men and women who will stand in the gap between them and the churches; men and women who will take the place of the minister here, because these people are prejudiced against the minister and will not listen to him. These people may be called missionaries or what you will, but we need them. They must go into these cottages to meet these people and teach them. Too often, though, we find men who can do nothing else, who are given this work of the Lord to do. We send them out to preach.

What we need is a training school for these people, that they may be taught and trained in their work. I know the need of this. I walked the streets of Chicago day after day, feeling that I must preach, yet knowing that I was not fitted for the work and wanted to learn. But I felt that to give up ten or twelve years to this preparation would be a sin. Had there been some place where I could have been trained and allowed to study, while I was at work I could have been more successful. We need such schools.

Then the preacher needs another school than that of theology. He needs to be trained in the school of human nature. They need to rub up against the world and learn how to read men. They fail to get hold of men for this very reason. Had they been business men and learned something of the world, or had they been like these reporters, seeing all sides of life, they would have known something of the other side and how to approach men. We want a training school to educate just such men for this work. In New York the other day I was speaking of this to a gentleman, and he said, all right, Mr. Moody you start such a school, and here is $5,000 to help with the work.

He made me take it, and when I came to Chicago another business man added $5,000 to it, and said start it here. That is what I say. Let Chicago have a training school for these men and women, and if there are any more of you gentlemen and ladies who want to contribute to such a work, come on with your money. I have been blamed for going away from Chicago; now if you want me to return give me some such work to do. We should have 200 or 300 men and women at work with the lower classes of people here in Chicago. I tell you it will pay. In London they have a thousand, and they are men and women, many of them who have not only given their wealth but themselves to the work. Some of the ladies are wealthy, yet they devote their lives to going about among these people and doing good. In this country our people are willing to serve the Lord by proxy. They are willing to spend their money, but not to work. I say to the rich men of Chicago, their money will not be worth much if communism and infidelity sweep the land. You had better lift up these men, and the best way is to take some from their own number. Some of our brightest men are in the billiard halls. Let us get this thing started.

I should like to have something practical grow out of this convention. We shall be here for three days and have a glorious time, and shout over it, and say let's have another one next year. It will last just for one year. But is that all? We can do so much more. We can do something that will be lasting in its results. There is no reason why these people should not be reached. But you are not going to reach them by a few sermons. The time has come when we will have to go into these people's homes and work. The church has been on the defensive long enough. It is time she was beginning an aggressive movement. We have lawyers who are eloquent in their pleadings in the courts. Why should they not plead in other places for these people? The work cannot be done by the ministers alone. We want the lawyers and the business men—all classes of men and women to go into the work, but especially we need a trained band of laborers to reach the lower classes.

The outlying homes will be reached quicker by this than by the preachers. You say these men have not logic. No matter. Let men preach for souls, not heads. If a man has not logic and cannot be appealed to by reason, drive straight at his heart. I like heart-preaching better, any way.

A few years ago a gentleman in London invited me to go down to the dog market. I asked him what that was, and found that it was a place where these rough men congregated on Sunday morning, and if they had anything to sell or trade or bet on for drinks they went there.

Well, we went to the dog market, and as I looked out at them it seemed there were acres of men—men rough and cursing, men with dogs to sell or to bet on as fighters; men with fighting cocks betting on them. It was one of the queerest sights I ever saw. And I was to-day to speak to them. They paid no attention until it was announced that I was an American. Then they listened to me for a few moments, because they had an idea that America was a sort of fairy land. But while I spoke a man stood at my side with a fighting cock under his arm, trying to hear what I was saying, but at the same time looking out to see if he could find another cock to match his against in a fight; and another man jostled me, trying to be a respectful listener, had a sharp lookout for a chance to get up a dog fight. And all there were, if listening to me, at the same time looking out for business in some shape, and my talk had no effect on them. But a blacksmith was able to interest them, and I say that is what we need. Let us use all kinds of talent. If we can put such men into training schools, and prepare them for teaching their fellows, we will do a grand work. It is practical and can be carried out here in Chicago better than in any city in the country.

"What is the best thing to do with a man who always speaks on one subject?"

These men are more numerous than you think. They are hobbyists. They do a good deal of harm, too. They break up many good meetings by presenting their hobbies at the wrong time. If a solemn impression has been made they will spoil it by presenting their hobby. I don't say that these are not good men, but they do much harm. I would try to keep them quiet by gentle means, if possible, but under no consideration would I allow them to go on. If they would not keep quiet for asking I should make them. I like temperance, but I don't want to talk about it all the time, and I like the doctrine of sanctification, but I don't want to hear of that and nothing else. It brings these good old doctrines into disrepute such harping on them. If I take my watch to the jeweler and ask to have the balance-wheel made double its present size, I am told that it will ruin the watch, for all the other machinery will then be out of proportion. Take any doctrine of the Bible and put it above every other and it will die.

"How are the foreign population to be reached?" Mr. Moody said it had been his privilege to go to Paris and see the work of one man there who did not understand the French language, and for a long time had to speak through an interpreter. This man had had a beautiful home, which he left, and himself and wife devoted themselves to the work of evangelization in Paris. He had worked steadily for years, and now he could speak a little very bad French, but he had a hall larger than Farwell Hall, Chicago, which was always crowded, and no man in Paris could draw a greater crowd to hear him speak than this evangelist. Mr. Moody had himself spoken to these people through an interpreter, and he thought it was a terrible dull talk, and he wondered that the people did not all rush out of the hall, but when he got through they remained, and when he invited a few to remain and hear about how to live a Christian life, they all remained while he preached another sermon. Then when he invited those who could to remain to talk about soul saving, they all remained, and he could not get them to go home until the gas was turned off, and they left in the dark. The foreigners were eager to hear the gospel. And here in Chicago we did not have to go to France or Germany or Sweden to find them. They come to us, and the best way to reach the foreigners was to train those here and send them as teachers to their native lands.

It was especially a good time to revive the religion of Christ in Germany this year, when the 400th anniversary of Martin Luther was to be celebrated. He then spoke of the work of an evangelist in Berlin who had been recognized by the Crown Prince and Prince

Bismarck. The doors of the nations were opened to us, and it was time to enter and possess.

"Do you think it is best to have steady work in the church, or revivals?"

"Both. Some people oppose revivals and preach against them, and they do a great harm. The church was born in a revival."

Mr. Moody then spoke of those people who are always crying out against revivalists, and evangelists. He told the story of the man who said at a dinner-table, when a missionary convert was present, that in all his travels in Asia he had never seen a native convert. The missionary did not reply, but after a while asked if he had ever seen a tiger there. The man replied that he had seen many, had hunted and killed them. The missionary's reply was that he had never seen a tiger while abroad. He had been hunting for converts, and not tigers.

We could find converts if we hunted for them, but the converts were not going to come round and ring the bell to let us know they were converted.

There were several other questions in the box, but it was 5 o'clock, and Mr. Moody is prompt in closing as in beginning, and announcing the doxology, it was sung, and the convention adjourned until 8 o'clock.

EVENING SESSION.

If the interest of the people in the afternoon amounted to a certain degree of absorption, the interest in the proceedings of the evening was to a still greater degree intensified

The exercises being opened in the usual way, Mr. Moody announced the topic for discussion, and the first speaker of the evening:

"HOW TO REACH HABITUAL NON-CHURCH GOERS."

Rev. Dr. H. M. Scudder, pastor of Plymouth Congregational Church, Chicago.

Dr. Scudder said:

Several answers may be given to this question. There are advocates of various schemes. Some say "Establish gospel services on Sunday evenings in halls and theatres." Others say, "Try to reach destitute populations through mission schools." Others call for street preaching. Others advise more extensive efforts on the part of Young Men's Christian Associations. And the most recent reply is: "Do it by Salvation Armies." I will not enter upon the consideration of any of these, but will give an answer, which, while it interferes with none of these, seems to me to be one of the most important things which can be said in reply to the question, viz: Make the sanctuary itself so attractive as to draw men into it.

Who shall do this? Not ministers alone. Not laymen alone. Either attempting it singly will fail, at least in a measure. If both heartily combine, there will be success. This Christian Convention consists of ministers and laymen, and I will venture to offer on this subject a few suggestions to each.

What shall ministers do to make the church attractive? In treating this, my dear brethren, I hope you will not think that I assume to be your teacher. I have no such spirit. The directions I give are rules unto myself. They may be useful to you, as I know they are to me.

There are some things ministers should not do. In order to avoid stiffness kindly allow me to use the second person in addressing you.

1. Do not make your sermons too doctrinal in form. Do not misunderstand me. A sermon without doctrine is good for nothing. It would be like a body without a backbone. There must be a backbone to give points of attachment for the limbs, to support the vital organs that are clustered around it, and to sustain the masses of muscles which execute so many motions. But if the body were all backbone and nothing else, it would not be a very agreeable spectacle. If when you looked for a body to meet you, you saw only a bare backbone approaching, you would run away from it. There must be a backbone, but over it should be the comely vesture of ruddy flesh, and at the top of it a living brain. In a sermon the doctrine should be clothed, as in the body God has clothed the backbone.

2. Do not let the sermon become a mere essay. It should be something other than a pretty, elaborate, finical, symmetrical essay. It may be poetic and polished, artistic and æsthetic, and quite beautiful to behold, and yet the people will soon grow weary of such preaching.

3. Do not overweight your sermon with learning. Iron is the most useful of metals, and it is proper that ships should carry it from country to country, to give it universal currency, that it may be applied to uses innumerable. But if you overload your vessel with iron till it sinks to its deck, and then spread your sails, and attempt a voyage, your ship, though a good one, will go to the bottom, iron and all, and you will be lucky if you yourself escape. Some sermons do not float, but go down overfreighted with learning.

Not that the minister can have too much learning. Christ has described the New Testament minister as a "scribe which is instructed unto the kingdom of heaven." The word "scribe" had in that day, a very different meaning from that which it now has. It meant a "learned man." Such the minister should be. It would be well if he knew everything, and had it at the end of his tongue.

But he must be wise in using his learning. Results should appear rather than processes. There should be no parade of learning. The sermon which merely carries a cargo of erudition is a doomed ship. It will not discharge its cargo in the port which the author of the sermon should steer for, but on the floor of the ocean.

Avoid sameness and repetitiousness. We sometimes hear such complaints as these: "Oh, he has a new text, but yet it will be the old sermon over again. We have heard it a hundred times. We are tired of it." Our Lord says that the minister must bring forth "out of his treasure things new and old." He must possess a treasure of acquisitions, and out of it must come new as well as old. Also our Master has said, "When ye pray use not vain repetitions." and this injunction may rationally be extended so as to read, "When ye preach, use not vain repetitions."

Let us turn from the negative to the positive. What shall ministers do to make their ministrations attractive?

1. Let there be more expository preaching. I feel sure that there is not enough of this done. Make your sermon an exposition of Holy Scripture. I do not mean that you should take up a chapter or a paragraph and explain it verse by verse, and word by word. What I mean is this: Choose a chapter or a passage which has impressed you. With a few sheets of paper before you, sit down at your desk, and study the passage carefully in the original; for if possible, every man who expounds Scripture should know Hebrew and Greek. When I was in the theological seminary I sat under the teaching of Dr. Edward Robinson, and a remark of his has had a very potent influence upon my life as a student.

He said, "Young gentlemen, they who teach the Bible, should be able to read it in the languages in which the Holy Ghost revealed it." And if I knew nothing of Hebrew and Greek I would, on going home from this meeting to-night, begin with Aleph and Alpha; and I rejoice in the work that Professor Harper has been doing in this city this summer in organizing classes for the reading of Hebrew.

Open then your Hebrew or Greek Lexicon according as your selected passage is in the Old or New Testament. Scrutinize every word; run each word through all its senses in the lexicon, and as you do this write down every thought and every illustration that comes into your mind. Do not aim, in this stage of your work, at any order. Set down every idea as it arises in you. The roots of the Hebrew and Greek words used in the Bible are living things. Give them a chance in the soil of your intellect and heart, and there will be a crowd of branches and leaves and blossoms and fruit. Professor Guyot, of Princeton College is a Hebrew scholar as well as a geologist! I heard him say many years ago that the roots of the Hebrew words used in the first chapter of Genesis to describe the cosmogony there recorded, were living geologic germs, carrying within them ideas which if stated could not have been understood, but which, now that the time is come, verify themselves in the discoveries of geology. When you have gone through the passage and written down all that the examination of the original words has suggested, you will find that you have rich materials, in abundance, for a sermon. Now reduce these materials to order.

Look for the central thought of the passage. Seize upon it. Select the verse that presents it—that central thought. Make that your text. Arrange all the other thoughts as satellites around this central thought and you will find that your sermon is rising up before you as a solar system, with its sun at the center, and planets and asteroids moving around it in light and warmth and harmony and beauty. It will not appear to be an expository sermon, but it will be such in the highest and best sense of that word. You may say that this will involve much time and toil, but a sermon ought to cost us something, and if we follow this plan of work we shall learn to do it with increasing rapidity and facility; with much fervor of mind and gladness of heart. And I would make expository preaching include the exposition of the volume of nature. Holy Scripture and nature are God's two great books, and the truths of Scripture have their analogies in nature. Have you a Scripture truth in hand? Search for its analogy in nature. The pursuit will be a delight, the discovery a joy, the appropriation an enrichment. And, having discovered it, illustrate the Scripture-truth by this, its embodiment which you have found in nature. Your hearers will never forget a truth so exemplified. Modern science has opened up to us this realm of nature. It is now a library rather than a volume. Be at home in this library. Acquaint yourself with its departments, that you may be able to bring into view the material expressions of spiritual truths.

A sermon thus constructed will be an expository discourse. It will be fresh, vivid, instructive, interesting, and so far as it catches the spirit which dwells in the Scripture and in nature it will be spiritual and divine. It will be a sermon that has sprung up, not out of one's own shallowness, but out of the great depths of God's mind and heart.

2. Let the manner of your utterance be colloquial. In the pulpit the simply natural is to be preferred to the rhetorical or the oratorical. Talk to your audience. Speak to them as you would to individuals in your own parlor. Unify your congregation so that it shall stand before you as a single person with whom you are about to argue and plead; whom you desire to conciliate, convince,

and lead into the love and practice of the truth which you are inculcating.

3. Let the truth which you propose to preach first thoroughly master you. Men like to see exhibitions of power, and no manifestation of power is more impressive than the perceived dominance of a truth over the speaker who is proclaiming that truth. Let your theme completely subdue and possess and absorb your own soul. Come into the pulpit every Sabbath with a week's new illumination and a week's spiritual glow.

4. Concentrate your energies on your own church and parish. Ministers are called upon to do much exterior work. Do what you can of this, without neglecting your own sphere of labor. Let that be the limit. Beyond that, learn to say "No." Sacrifice, if needs be, outside popularity to inside usefulness. The minister who thus restricts, and disciplines and develops himself, will draw hearers to himself. He will have something to give, and men generally find their way to the place where they can get anything.

But though the minister fulfill this scheme of thought and preparation and action, his success will only be partial, if he has not the hearty co-operation of the members of his church.

What then shall laymen do to make the church attractive? There are three effective things they can do.

1. Set a good example in attending church yourselves. See how it is now in most churches. The members come in the morning. The house is full. But to a great extent they have abandoned the evening service. They require their minister to preach, as well as he can, to empty pews, unless he can draw in strangers that shall occupy them. When these church members called this minister to be their leader they promised to support him. Instead of fulfilling their promise they break his heart by their absence. They tell him to lead, they call him their captain, they push him to the front, they put the banner of the church into one of his hands, and bid him take the sword of the Spirit, the Word of God in the other; and yet they who are his soldiers, who have vowed to stand by him, desert him, and from a distance, the distance of their respective homes, cry out to him and say: "Fight it out, be plucky, do not give in, be valiant; we admire what you are attempting." What can be more disheartening than this? It puts a burden upon the minister he cannot carry. He staggers under it. I was not long since in a church which has a distinguished, eloquent, devout and learned pastor. He has a good audience in the morning, and about a hundred in the evening. His health gave way last winter, and an officer in his church said to me, "This was what broke him down."

How can we expect outsiders to come in, when the insiders set such an example of indifference and disloyalty? It is no wonder if people say: "Christians stay out, why should we go in?"

If the laymen would attend church in the evening as they do in the morning, the minister would be greatly encouraged. The presence of his people, the thought that they were praying for him, would be a stimulus to him. He would preach ten times better than he does.

2. Not only attend the services, but assume the right attitude toward strangers.

There is a tendency in the churches to degenerate into aristocratic religious clubs; a tendency to welcome the rich, and repel the poor. This is an evil spirit. Exorcise it. Open your pews freely. Open your hearts. If you see a stranger in the audience, go to him at the close of the service, speak a kind word to him, give him a cordial grasp of the hand. He will not forget it. He will come again. In a church where I was the other night, five young men were sitting in a pew in front of the deacon. When the service was over he went and shook hands with them all. They will remember that.

Honor the poor. Let the fact that you are better off than they lead you to pay them special attention. Do it, not as though it were an act of condescension, but with a loving heart. Choose as ushers your best men; the kindest, the aptest, the most courteous, the men who possess the most social qualities. Thus make the church as attractive as possible.

3. Let each member try to bring in some who are not accustomed to attend church. Do you know one such? Invite him. Set your heart on him, pray for him, go for him.

In order to accomplish any great achievement two things are needful. First, a definite purpose. Nothing worthy can be attained at hap-hazard. There must be an aim, a goal toward which we intelligently, resolutely, prayerfully, and persistently strive. Let this be the aim; let pastor and people unite in this determination: "We will fill our church with people, and by God's grace endeavor to convert all that come into it."

And there is a second thing, for, though we propose this to ourselves, we shall not succeed without enthusiasm. Revert to the origin of this word which means "inspired by God," "full of God." Christ is our God. He is our Immanuel, God with us. But He must be even more than that to us. He must be Christ in us, dwelling in us by His holy spirit quickening, guiding, and sustaining us. This is the divine baptism, perpetual and effective. If we have this, the church will be attractive, and it will become the place where many souls shall be reborn.

The succeeding feature of the evening's session was the singing of the "Song of the Soldier" by the male choir. It had a sturdy, martial ring, worthy of soldiers of the cross; so much so that Mr. Moody sprang up—and the spirit that moves Mr. Moody is an awfully active one—and exclaimed, in his blunt, honest way, that that was the way to reach non-church-goers, by a male choir. He liked that singing, he said; he liked it better than speaking anyway. Then incidentally he told of the success in training enjoyed by certain bands of men in Glasgow whose voices at first were simply execrable, but which proved susceptible of such improvement that, after a time, their worthy owners were mighty factors in drawing large audiences to this and that building in the city of Glasgow by the power and tunefulness of their cultivated voices. So Mr. Moody had reason to applaud the good work of the choir at his elbow, and demand, with his little fling at the speakers, while laughter arose, another hymn from his staunch auxiliaries and his audience combined.

Following Dr. Scudder there were appointed as speakers the Rev. Bishop C. E. Cheney, and the Rev. M. M. Parkhurst. Rev. Dr. Parkhurst began by saying that he supposed that ministers had studied the question from the beginning of their work, and it had been as much a question of thought and work as any other. The class of people to reach in the consideration of the question was the non-church-going one. The convention had been told that 95 per cent. of the workingmen of Manchester did not go to church. We would find that this number was increasing about us. It was a hard thing to break down the habit of non-church-going. There is, in the first place, a prejudice on the part of this class to encounter. They feel that they do not know the people who attend the churches, and that the church is not their social club.

There were people in the city who did not know whether the church in their block was Protestant or Catholic, German or English. One could hardly believe that such a thing existed, yet it was true. One of the first things to do was to break down the prejudice entertained by this class that ministers were mere hirelings, acting in a perfunctory way. An incident was related that occurred at the Annapolis naval school during the war. An order was issued one morning to all the men to attend service. There were sixty Roman Catholics who refused to obey an order, as they understood it, to attend a service outside their own church. The commander said they would have to go, or suffer the consequences of a disobedience of orders. The speaker said that there was a chance for a fight and trouble. He went to a Catholic priest, and, telling him what had taken place, asked him if he could not arrange to have these men attend a service conducted according to their own belief. The reply was, certainly, and a service was held. The men attended and found that places had been reserved for them in the church.

When they returned they felt pleased, and in the afternoon they gladly turned out to hear the speaker preach, and said that they would always be ready to hear him. By kindness their prejudices had been overcome.

The speaker had found that funerals afforded a good opportunity, and while the hearts of those present were still warm, and before the tears were wiped away he had something to say that would draw them to the church. At weddings, too, there was an opportunity to say something. An excellent means of bringing outsiders into the church was the visiting of ladies among the people in following and working up any particular movement.

He suggested that a lesson could be learned from the shrewd business man in his efforts to reach the people. He was constantly advertising. When his sales have reached millions why not stop advertising? He knew that when he dropped out of the public eye his business did so too.

The force of this was illustrated by relating an experience in the First M. E. Church. When he was first connected with it he found that but about eighty persons attended the Sunday night services. He had 5,000 circulars printed for distribution every Saturday night, announcing the service of the evening following. There was not a store, or restaurant, or place into which they did not find their way. The result of this constant and consistent advertising was that in a year's time the attendance increased to 400. It was hard work, and could be accomplished only by hard and constant hammering. Besides there must be workers to follow this up.

Similar incidents were related. In a shoe-making suburb of Boston, of 5,000 people there were no church-goers. Every Saturday night texts were distributed through the shops, "Remember to keep holy the Sabbath," among others. In three years there was a church of over 700. The Baptists followed, and then the Unitarians in the work.

At Elgin, on the west side of the river, there was a population of 3,500, practically none of them church-goers. A young man was stationed among them and told to go to work. In eleven months a Sunday school with a regular attendance of 500 was built up.

Get hold of the people and attract them to the church. Build up a fire, and where there was a fire there would be a crowd. Nobody cared to gather about a cold stove. Kindle in your hearts the fire of the love of God. You must have warmth or you will freeze.

The great trouble was that enough work was not done. He wanted to see the fire and warmth of this great convention go out through the city and the Northwest.

After a hymn by the choir, and prayer by Dr. Savage, Bishop Cheney was called upon by Mr. Moody to speak on the same topic. Bishop Cheney said: He confessed that he was appalled when he stood before the vast audience, not appalled at the audience, but at his ability to pack in ten minutes' time the thought involved in this question.

He wanted to draw a clear and distinct definition. First of all, to reach and influence the hearts of those outside, there must be a revival in the church. It had been well said that there was a prejudice against the church, and the pride of church members, and the coldness of the ministers were complained of by outsiders. Was it not time that the church needed an outpouring of the spirit that would kindle the fire of love? There was need of a quickening of the hearts and souls of the professed Christian, that would make them consistent followers of Christ, so that when one of them passes by it could be said, There is a Christian man, or woman. When that point was reached the professed Christian would be able to extend his influence over those outside.

There was need of personal effort. He indorsed everything that had been said about the thorough advertising and meetings and services, and about the efforts to build up evening services. The great trouble was that not enough effort was made to reach the individual, but all was directed toward the masses.

The masses could only be reached through the individual first. He believed that a great mistake had been made by the churches on this question. The great question was, "How can I reach the individual?" We want more individual effort, and on the part of the layman above all things else. If we are to reach and touch the souls that habitually neglect the gospel, we must give them something that they cannot get in any other place. Tell the old story of the gospel. Christ crucified alone touched and influenced man.

SECOND DAY OF THE CONVENTION.

MORNING SERVICE.

The second day of the Christian convention was as largely attended as the first, and as early as eight o'clock there were hundreds of people seeking admission to Farwell Hall, that they might secure eligible seats, and at nine o'clock all the seats on the first floor were taken, and many in the gallery.

"HOW SHALL WE SECURE A LARGER ATTENDANCE AT PUBLIC WORSHIP?"

Rev. P. S. Henson, D. D., pastor of the First Baptist Church, Chicago, addressed the audience as follows:

I might speak to you of a score of points, each one of which would be helpful in its measure to secure the object contemplated in this question, but I shall speak of only a few that suggest themselves to me, and I pray that God will help me to emphasize these few as their supreme importance demands.

And, first of all, allow me to say, for it is on my heart, and in it, that in order to secure a larger attendance of people upon public worship, there should be Sunday-school training of the children in the direction of attendance on the preaching of the gospel. The first thing to be done is in the sphere of the Sunday-school. I thank God that I live in the foremost age of human history, for I am not one of those who are continually inquiring why the former days were better that these. I believe these to be the best days the world has ever seen, and I thankful for the realization in our time of the Scriptures saying, "A little child shall lead them." Yet I cannot ignore the fact that in connection with mighty movements in God's kingdom there are always present occasions of peril. There is a disposition to the divorcement of that which God joined together, and man was never meant to put asunder.

In former times parents took their children with them to the house of God, and sat with them to listen to the ministrations of the Gospel, but now the tendency is to post the children off to the children's service, while the poor pastor is likely to be left alone with a cold adult congregation from which the young life has ebbed away. If I am bereaved of my children I am bereaved indeed. So it follows that in many communities the Sunday-school bond with the church is broken, and that Sunday-school children, when they cease to be Sunday-school children, never having been in the habit of attending worship in their youth, are, of all classes, the most difficult to reach. I have no protests to make against the Sunday-school; for I have given the strength of my life to it, and shall ever continue to support it. I would not tear up the rails because of the dangers of railroad travel. I would not quench the fire in the locomotive, but would see to the switches, make sure of the bridges. Let superintendents and Sunday-school teachers see that the children in their charge are brought up to attend on the preaching of the word. If the alternative were to disband the Sunday-school or to have a separation of the children from the preaching service, I would say shut up the Sunday-schools for all time to come. But it is not necessary. Let us see to the church training. Let us bring our children with us to the house of God, I speak not as a Christian minister, but as a Christian man, profoundly solicitous for all the far-reaching interests of Christ's kingdom.

There must not only be Sunday-school training, but more personal solicitation. There is an idea widely prevalent that our churches are select and exclusive; that they are religious clubs; that they are concerned alone with their own enjoyment; that they are out of sympathy with general humanity. This is not true. There is not a minister on the platform here who would not rejoice in a crowd. Mr. Moody is not the only one who likes a crowd. Where is there a minister whose heart would not rejoice and whose eye would not glisten at the incoming of the masses? Our hearts yearn for them, and yet there is a presumption that the churches do not care to have them come; that the churches are close corporations; and, judging from the looks of many who join in pious procession to church with their prayer-books and hymn-books under their arms, unmindful, apparently, of the multitude around them, who are as sheep without a shepherd, the world has reason to believe that they do not care for the souls of their fellows. To dispossess men's minds of this false impression, we must go from house to house, and canvass the whole community, and give earnestness to our invitation. It is not sufficient to open the doors. Christ did not simply open an office at Jerusalem. He came to seek as well as save them that were lost. We must go after the masses and bring them in. There is wonderful meaning in the passage of Scripture which says, our Saviour took the man by the hand and led him out of town. We must take them by the hand and lead them into the house of God.

Not only must we have this and Sunday-school training, but

Christian living also. The great reason why many men do not go to church is the revulsion of disgust which comes to them from seeing the contrast between living and profession among those who do go to church. They look at the lives of church-going people and often see painful evidence that church-going does not avail to make them holier and happier; and so they say: "What is the use of attending church if one is not better for it?"

If I am broken down almost with constant strain of heart and brain, and I see men coming back in the crisp autumn time from sea-shore and mountain, bronzed and brawny, with new elasticity in every step, I say to myself, I, too, will drink health-giving waters; I will inhale the breezes of mountain air; I will riot in the surf, that I too may recover back the lost vigor of my life. So if God's people are seen to be the better for their going to church—if those who come forth from its doors are found to be more stalwart and pure in all life's relations, and if by manifestation of the truth they commend themselves to every man's conscience in the sight of God, then there will be streams of people pouring into God's house; for in the most degraded heart there are flashes of angelic beauty as well as traces of demoniac evil, a vague, vast longing for a better life; but men must first be made to believe in Christians before they can be made to believe in Christianity, or be brought to seek it in the house of God.

These things that I have spoken of are things outside. Then there must be things done inside if we would increase the attendance; and one of these is cordial, hearty welcoming. There is a great deal depending upon how a man is met at the church-door. I will not enter now at length upon that much mooted question of free churches versus rented pews. There are considerations that may be urged in behalf of both sides of the question. There are advantages in having it understood that every seat is free to everybody—free as the air and the light and the water that God gives. There are advantages in that. There are advantages also in the system which allows a whole family to go together, the little child nestling in God's house by the side of the parents; in having people gather in groups and circles as in the family. There is much to be said on both sides of this subject. But do you know that a man in a free church, who has come to preempt a seat by long occupation, may look as grim at any stranger, taking it as though he had paid a thousand dollars for it [laughter], while, on the other hand, a man may pay a thousand dollars for a pew, and he may make it free by the beaming smile, the joyousness, the hearty hospitality with which he asks you to take a seat in it. [Applause.] But whether a church be nominally free, or whether its revenues be raised by members taxing themselves by pew-rents, if a man rents a pew to hold it against all comers, I would not have him hold it a minute.

Then, again, I would have strangers met at the door by the best men that the church has—representative men, noble men—big-hearted men, who shall give to the stranger the best seat in the house. A great deal depends upon this cordial welcoming of strangers, and bidding them come again.

And then another thing is gospel preaching, and I say this because it needs to be said. There is a great deal of preaching done by those who do not deserve the name of preachers. Of course we all desire to do the best thing possible, but we are apt to be mistaken as to what is the best thing. In this age of culture and advanced thought, a minister may think that he must be fully posted in all that is in the latest books, and to tell it all to show his hearers that he is abreast of the age, and that they may be profoundly impressed with his stores of knowledge. I don't know anything about that kind of preaching, and I thank God for it. [Applause]. I remember preaching some sermons in answer to Tyndall. There were others answering him, and so I thought I must take my chance at him, and launch a polished shaft at him. And I did—not one, but many.

Coming out of the house one day, after one of these sermons, a big-brained, big-hearted man met me, laid his hand on my shoulder, and said: "We don't care a continental about that man that you have been preaching about to-day. [Laughter.] Preach Christ crucified and we shall enjoy it better." I replied, "May God forgive me, and I hope you will." And since then I have delivered all the scientists over to the special care of Jehovah. Talk about Tyndall! The biggest brained men in the community who come to occupy seats in your church do not care on the Lord's day about your logical concatenation of scientific arguments. They have hearts that want to be fed, and are full of infinite yearning after the old gospel. The old, old story is the newest thing out—the most beautiful thing below the shining stars. And that is the story to tell; that, the thing to preach. What were Christ's words? "If I be lifted up I will draw all men unto me." We must have the preaching that exalts Christ, that draws men to him—the plain, pungent preaching of the old truths that are infinitely deep and infinitely high and infinitely tender. These are the things that grapple with men's consciences; that get hold of men's heart strings and draw them to God. You may preach culture, politics, humanity; and you will soon wear them out, but the story of the gospel is as new to-day as when the Lord Jesus first proclaimed salvation on the hills of old Judea.

One thing more and I have done. I have spoken of Sunday-school training in its relation to church-going, of personal solicitation, of cordial welcoming, and of gospel preaching; and there is one more thing, and that is spiritual quickening. We hear much talk about men of magnetic power. We want men who will draw, and churches that will draw. What is anything good for unless it will draw; what is a chimney good for that will not draw, or a locomotive, or a man? [Laughter.] We want men who will draw. Some preachers, monotonous preachers, who don't draw, who never stir themselves nor others, protest against what they call sensational preaching. I believe in sensational preaching. A minister cannot indeed afford to make a mountebank of himself, because he is God's ambassador. He cannot descend to the juggler's tricks that are unworthy of the minister of Jesus Christ. But all great preachers that have stirred men's hearts were sensational. Jesus Christ and Paul and Martin Luther and Calvin were sensational. What you want is a man that will rouse men---a man that will draw. In order to draw, in order to have this magnetism, there must be the communication of the divine Spirit. A magnet may be made out of a piece of cold iron. You pass a coil of wire around it, called a helix, and then you turn on the electricity. The electricity sweeps around, and it is transformed into a magnet, and lifts and draws in a wonderful way.

Just so, if a preacher in the pulpit be compassed by this divine influence, this subtle power of the Spirit, if there be connection with the poles at the very throne of God, then he, too, will be a magnet; God having filled him with his own divine power. So on the day of Pentecost there came from heaven the sound of a rushing, mighty wind, and it filled the house. That is what we want. It filled the whole house where they were gathered, and the apostles were all filled with the Holy Ghost. And mark what followed. There were no placards on the wall, no advertisements in the newspapers, and yet it is recorded that just as soon as the Holy Spirit filled the place, the people from without came together. And that is the way to fill the house of God. The people will find it out. The tidings will fly like an electrical flash; and you will soon wonder where the multitudes come from. God sends them. And so the house is filled. And if we be thus filled with the divine spirit, this question of the filling of the house will have settled itself, and we shall have to lengthen the cords and strengthen the stakes and break out on the right hand and the left, for the place in which we dwell will be too strait for us; and all flesh will see the glory of our God. [Applause].

Mr. J. L. Houghteling, President of the Young Men's Christian Association, being introduced to continue, in a ten-minute talk, the subject of church attendance, prefaced his remarks by saying that his standpoint would be that of the pews, as Dr. Henson's had been from the pulpit. The newspapers said this morning, began he, that the Christian Convention was one of the greatest gatherings of Christian people that had ever been held. In the hall there were 3,000 people; outside, comprising the remainder of the city, were 647,000 others. Supposing that instead of Farwell Hall the Exposition Buildings were occupied for the same purpose, there would perhaps be a daily attendance of 10,000, aggregating in the three days 30,000. This latter total then, when compared with the population of the city would represent about the proportion of church goers. The reason for this small proportion of church-going people was found in the fact that through human corruption the church had come to be designed for the few in question. The church had become equivalent to a piece of merchandise, something with salable features, like a position on the Board of Trade. This was hard talk, remarked the speaker, but true. The facts of Christianity were neglected in the churches, and too much attention instead, given to theory. The people had gone back upon the facts, while to the pastor was left the theory.

"Let me picture the average church in Chicago," continued Mr. Houghteling, who forthwith sketched the reality most effectively. He said that all the pews were let out under a sense of proprietorship, and that there was no proneness to take in strangers. An invitation to attend church was published in the Sunday morning papers, with the invitation left out. When strangers from force of habit or conviction attended they were met by a parcel of well-dressed gentlemen, and could but observe that the service was of a character somewhat habitual and perfunctory, conducted under the belief that it would all improve one's chances of heaven. Was there any wonder that the proportion of church-goers was small?

The rented pew business, continued the speaker, who incidentally observed that he stood up from the pews, and so spoke for their occupants, was a modern business, and a system which he was inclined to say was one of the mistakes of Protestantism. He had found no recommendation in the Bible about high places in the synagogue. The pew-renting system was not found among Catholics, unless they had been corrupted by juxtaposition with Protestants.

In the great cathedrals abroad seats were free and room for prince and beggar, side by side.

The speaker declared himself not afraid to say that free churches were a very important element in drawing masses. Experience in Chicago had proven this true. There was a little church in this city where the seats were free as air—freer than water, for water was taxed. In this little church there was more money spent in the service of God than in any church of its size in all Chicago. Which the active little congregation was Mr. Houghteling refrained from publicly announcing, but expressed his willingness to tell, more privately, any and all.

In England it had been shown that the free churches were the ones that drew. Perhaps some might say that our churches can't be turned from proprietary to free churches. But the second service could be made free as air, and every Christian man could become a cordial host in the house of God. A cordial invitation should be extended to people. And how? Let some family in each block be named who should care for the interests of the stranger in that block and see that they are invited to attend this or that church as the denomination and locality of the family might be; while if the stranger were of a denomination not identical with this particular family, then the latter should inform the pastor of that other denomination that such and such people are within his jurisdiction. In this way should the interests of parishioners be followed up, nor need there either, at the same time, be any machinery in it.

Another element of attraction to churches, and a factor for good, was successful ushering. Besides the Spirit of Almighty God a cordial manner and common sense were essential characteristics of an usher. He should be honestly glad to see a person, and should welcome him as his best friend and in his own house. Again, an usher should use discretion in the locating of strangers in church pews. A poor mother, just from the washing of her dishes, and clad in a humble way, would feel uncomfortable in a front seat where she might feel that the entire attention of the congregation was attracted toward herself. Then, again, good judgment should so far direct an usher that he would not place a modest young country lad in the same pew with a young lady. He certainly wouldn't feel at home, and it wasn't altogether certain that she would be particularly pleased.

Speaking from personal information Mr. Houghteling alluded to the pronounced success achieved by one good church officer whose cordiality and sincerity of manner eventually brought into his church seventy young men, who came to stand shoulder by shoulder to worship.

Let the churches be made as free as grace, as free as his call who had said come all and be refreshed. Let the facts of Christianity be brought up to its theories, and the churches would be filled.

At the conclusion of Mr. Houghteling's remarks, Mr. Moody said if all these advocates of free churches would come over to Chicago Avenue they would be given seats. As Dr. Henson said, there were two sides to this question. There was a class of people who wanted to be together in church as a family. These should have some consideration. When in London he had made inquiry regarding the management of Mr. Spurgeon's church. He found that the pews there were rented, but the highest-priced pew was 7s. 6d. or about $2 in our money for the quarter, or $8 a year. Thus the very best seat in the tabernacle could be purchased by the poorest laboring man to hear the grandest man on the face of the globe. The cheapest pew was about one-fourth this amount. If we could not have free churches, we could have them with pews at a price within the reach of every one. They could make a compromise.

The hymn "Bringing in the Sheaves" was sung, and Major Whittle led in prayer.

The quartette on the platform sang "Peace, Be Still."

Dr. Ninde, of the Garrett Biblical Institute at Evanston, then took up the topic:

"HOW CAN THE INFLUENCE OF CHRISTIAN HOMES BE INCREASED?"

He commenced by saying that he felt both oppressed and stimulated by the magnitude of the theme. He doubted if there was a more important theme in the programme, however inadequate the discussion might prove. The union of the hearts by the marriage tie constituted the home; the indissoluble union of the Christian hearts constituted the Christian home. How can the influence of such a home be increased?

1. By increasing the attractiveness of the home in its natural features. Amid the havoc and wreck which sin had made the home is the oasis in our social desert. Missionaries speak of the heathen women as looking in through the doors of Christian dwellings and weeping as they contrasted the barrenness and misery of their own. By seeking to make our home life warm and genial and beautiful, we indirectly but powerfully increase its influence for religious ends.

2. We may increase the influence of the home for religious ends by deepening our conviction of the great idea for which the home was founded. God's purpose in the home was to seek thereby a godly seed. The religious nurture of childhood is therefore the grand work of Christian parents. And to effect this purpose we need to revive the old and faded truth of the church in the house. We are too apt to associate God's special presence and Christian work too exclusively with the temple where the Christian community gather for religious worship, and forget that this earth has no more sacred place than the dwelling consecrated by the devotion of loving hearts.

It is a glorious privilege, amid the religious indifference of these times, to stand within one's own threshold a divinely anointed representative of the family, and declare that, "as for me and my house, we will serve the Lord." The great work of Christian parents is to create, instrumentally, and nurture piety in their children. This work must be done promptly. The work must begin even before the dawn of self-consciousness. To delay is to lose the best opportunity and to imperil the souls of our children. It must be pursued continuously. God never wavers in His gracious work. At no moment is He absent from the heart of the child. It must be done with infinite painstaking. No press of worldly cares must interfere with our unwavering devotion to the religious welfare of our children. And the discipline we employ must be largely self-discipline. There is an unconscious influence which goes out from our very tones and looks and powerfully modifies the character of the young.

Such painstaking care will lead to a holy tact in presenting religion to our children. We shall present religion, not by obtruding, but by insinuating it. We too often preach to our children. We assail and overwhelm them with it, and thus too often arouse their prejudices and defeat our purest wishes. To expend care now is to save ourselves care in the future. The worst furies that lash the soul of many a father and mother are the living or dead victims of parental neglect.

3. The influence of Christian homes may be vastly increased over those who are its transient inmates. Many a one has felt a strange impressiveness in the very atmosphere of a pious home leading him to Christ. The Christian home ought to be signalized by gracious, saving influences upon all who enter within its sphere.

Rev. Dr. Hatfield followed Dr. Ninde in the discussion of this topic, and said it was the most important question that had been before the convention. But one might better try to preach ten sermons on it than deal with it in ten minutes. He had read an article in one of the popular quarterlies on "The Dangerous Classes." He had supposed that this referred to the tramps and communists, but was surprised to find that it referred to the wealthy men—the men who were in the great corporations, the monopolists, as the dangerous classes, and he quite agreed with the writer, Dr. Howard Crosby, or at least thought he was not far out of the way. He agreed with others that every soul saved was of equal value before God. When we become enthusiastic in caring for the neglected classes we were in danger of missing a great class very much in need. He had been making observations for years regarding the history and future of children of prominent members of the Christian churches, and he stood appalled at the facts that confronted him.

He had stood in the churches and looked at the leading men there—men whose names were good for thousands—men who had been in the church for years, and yet not one of them had a son worthy his weight in scrap iron, so far as religion was concerned. He had gone to other congregations and found the same thing there. He had looked over the churches in this city, and he declared that it was a rare thing to find a man of prominence there who has a son in the work of Christ. Many of these sons were worldly, not a few were skeptical and atheistic. Many were steeped in crime to the very lips, and they were bringing their fathers and mothers down to the grave in sorrow. It was not so bad on the other side of the house, but the daughters were living lives of pleasure. What was the matter? He was afraid he would not pass a very good examination in the doctrine of election, and he would no doubt be pronounced unorthodox, but he believed in the election of the sons and daughters of Christian parents as much as he believed in the election of any one. He could look over families and predict their home life. He knew of a moral certainty that the children would be found at the Savior's feet. In the house of God one would see the father, mother, sons and daughters all go to the table and partake of the sacrament. Then there were other families where it was just as clear to his mind that there would be slight gleaning for Christ. What was the matter, he asked? What was to be done to increase the power for Christ in the homes? If they had to go through the process of converting people over and over, and could never plant missions where the children would be brought into the church by the influence of the home, they could not expect to save the world to Christ.

He believed in a gospel that saved men, and he believed in employing all classes, but he had not so much faith in that kind of work that wanted to save alone the drunkard and the prize-fighter and other men of the vicious classes. He believed in saving the homes and the children who were born to God in Christian homes. He believed in reclaiming the heathen, but there were the children of the church to be saved and they must not be neglected. He had often thought of what must have been the thoughts of our first mother, Eve, with her first child. She had no mother to instruct her in raising her child. He had something of the same feeling as he looked upon the young mother to-day with her babe in her arms. He paid a glowing tribute to the Christian mothers of the land who were doing so much for character in the rising generations.

The first thing needed in this work was character on the part of the parents, and especially on the part of the mothers. Something in the way of reproof might be necessary, but the thing that environed the child from its infancy was the kindly influence of Christian parents. He knew of one house where there were nine children, and they could as men and women all testify to the fact that they had never heard an angry word or received an angry look from the Christian mother who presided over that home. And her work was seen in the Christian character of the sons and daughters left to revere her memory. God's blessing rested upon that family.

What could be done for the mothers especially? One thing was of great and all-absorbing importance. The mothers should be thoroughly convinced of the importance of the work given them to do. He might be old-fogyish on this subject, but he was not carried away by the idea of sphere in woman's work.

He believed the highest sphere for woman was in the home as the mothers of families. He had heard one member of the convention remark that the husbands in his church stayed at home and took care of the children while their wives were out doing the church work. He preferred that his wife should remain at home where she had so much influence for good in molding the character of the children. He said a man might go on the Board of Trade and be greatly impressed with the magnitude of the business transacted there, but for him he believed that the work of the wives at home was a hundred times more important than this. Yes, the mothers were doing a grander work and were of more importance than the President of the United States. In speaking of church going he said he did not believe in holy-day Christians—people who were exhausted with one service, for whom one sermon was too much to digest. They spent their afternoons reading the Sunday papers or riding on the boulevards. The children were sent to Sabbath-school, but for his part he preferred that his children should not be sent to the Sunday school at the sacrifice of the preaching service. There was in every man a fool age—the age when a youth was neither boy nor man, but knew more than his father or mother or the ancients, and he was too big to go to Sunday school. Had he been trained in going to church the church would have some hold upon him, but he had not and he was lost to the influences that the church might have been able to throw around him.

These children of the Sabbath school were the ones who neglected the church in their later years. They should be taken into the church and made to feel at home there. In his own home it had never been a question of going to church on Sunday morning any more than it was as to whether the children should eat their breakfast Monday morning or go to school. It was the order of the household and everybody conformed to it.

He spoke also of Bible instruction, and regarded the mothers as the best instructors. The mother had the children for seven days in the week, and the Sunday school for one hour. In Sabbath observance he found that the mothers had a great influence upon the children. He had a word for the men who were "compelled" to work on Sunday, and said no man was compelled. No man was compelled to own stock in the companies that were breaking the Sabbath. "Give it to them," came from the rear of the platform, and the Doctor went on for a moment more pouring hot shot at the corporations that indulged in Sabbath breaking.

Mr. Moody took the floor as soon as it was released by Dr. Hatfield and said he would subscribe to most that he had said, but he wanted him to pitch into the fathers as well as the mothers.

He then told how he had cornered a good Christian into confessing that he had spent every evening away from home—no matter if it was at prayer-meeting and church services—was away during all the day, and never saw anything of his children, and yet he grieved that his children had wandered away from him. No man had a right to do this. No minister had a right to give up seven evenings during the week and reserve none for his family. For himself he always reserved Saturday and evening for his wife and children, and was very cross if asked to give up that day to any other purpose. He thought every man should do this much at least for his family, that he might get acquainted with his children.

AFTERNOON SESSION.

Mr. Moody introduced the first subject and speaker of the afternoon.

"DEVOTIONAL EXERCISES."

Rev. Dr. W. M. Lawrence, Pastor of Second Baptist Church, Chicago, spoke as follows:

If comparisons are allowable, this question may be considered as one of the most important ones presented in the schedule. It is certainly one of the most difficult anywhere, but especially in this city and vicinity, and in attempting to answer it I would say, first, in our plan of work give the devotional meetings the place they are given in the word of God. I understand by devotional meetings the prayer gatherings, and I suppose that every minister and Christian workman has some sort of plan or some set of principles running through his work. His preaching service comes in for some part, his pastoral work comes in for another, his benevolent work for another, his public work for another, and his devotional work for another. If, then, these are to work in peace and profit, let him adjust them and prepare for them as God's word—his chart indicates.

I think you will appreciate this point better if you consider the prevailing notions men possess who appear not to have studied this phase of Christ's work. Go into the majority of our churches, and what do you find? A spacious audience room, carefully ventilated, ample preparation for excellent music, seats that are comfortable, the whole place easy of access, and in every way, inviting. Now, what next? Up a long alley and at the back of the building, or down cellar, or in the middle of the church is a room half the size, seldom as large as that, is what is called the prayer room.

Sometimes it is in deplorable condition. It is so low ceiling it is impossible to ventilate it. As a rule I do not believe in building chapels and then the main audience rooms, but I have sometimes thought it well to let it be done because the people might in that way get a good prayer room. The common idea about the whole thing is that it is a second-rate affair.

Even the minister's conducting of the affair is looked upon and expected to be a second-rate affair, a slovenly affair. And architecture and service combine to teach the people that the devotional services are secondary, and, like certain physician's prescriptions, may be taken or omitted at pleasure, and they literally are. Now if you want to have the meetings more profitable you must kill the prevailing notion regarding them, and this can be done as I have stated, by showing what position such meetings have in God's word.

And they are recognized therein. If you want a commentary on the prayer meeting take the Book of Acts. Before you get through the first chapter you have two prayer meetings. The first, a meeting for consolation right after our Lord's departure. These all continued with one accord in prayer and supplication with the women and Mary, the mother of Jesus, was there and His brethren. And the second was to ask advice about choosing a successor to Judas.

Take the next chapter. They are again gathered in an upper room, and suddenly there came a sound of a rushing, mighty wind. The Holy Ghost came, and the Church of the Apostolic day was born, 3,000 men were born, and where the characteristics of the converts are given in the close of the chapter it is said that they all remained steadfast in the Apostle's doctrine and fellowship, and in breaking of bread and prayers. So the fourth chapter tells how, after the release of Peter and John, they went to their own company and had prayer and a new baptism and the Holy Ghost. And you will not forget that after the release of Peter by the angel he came down to where they had a prayer-meeting, and they could not believe that the object of the prayer-meeting had been accomplished so soon, and refused to believe Rhoda that Peter was at the door. And then do not forget that woman's gathering at the place for prayer where the European church was born, in the heart of Lydia, and gather together these instances, and tell me if God's word assigns to the prayer gathering any such secondary idea that is so common to-day. We elevate the sermon as though it were the only way to reach a human heart; but the sermon is the testimony of but one man; the prayer-meeting, the testimony of many.

2. Give it the place in your church work that it has had in the experience of successful Christians. Where are men converted in the prayer-room? It is true they are convicted under the preaching—most of them, but the sun that ripens this fruit is a prayer-meeting. It may be of two only. But the Lord is there.

> "And heaven comes down our souls to greet,
> And glory crowns the mercy seat."

I heard recently that all the while Finney was preaching he had a man out praying for him. When our brethren who are with us to-day were in Philadelphia the meetings of power were the prayer-meetings, and observe the moments of power at this session have been the moments which we have spent before the cross. Teach your people in every way that church success is prayer-meeting success; that they cannot succeed without it. Teach them what place it holds in the economy of church labor, and when you have reproved the false ideas regarding its importance you have gone a long ways towards making them interesting.

3. Give the people clear ideas of what a devotional meeting is. If it is anything it has a purpose in it. They are called sometimes "social" meetings of the church, but "social" should be characteristic of all your gatherings. But the social part of a prayer-meeting is apt to come when the benediction has been pronounced, and people go to get a little dry religion and look out for a pleasant time afterward. They are devotional meetings—meetings where all the people give themselves into the hands of the Lord, to realize His presence. They are meetings for conversation, for confession of Christ, for confession of sin. They are the family meetings of the church, where plans of work are to be broached and God's wisdom invoked.

4. They are the people's meetings.

Let the leader, whoever he may be, remember that his place is guide. Especially let him consider this in the selection of his topic, so that it shall have some relation to the life of his people that week. To engage the attention of the people upon the condition of the inhabitants of Alaska, when God is pouring out His Spirit upon the Sunday-school is folly. Let the topic be born out of the very life of the people. Let the condition of the church give rise to the topic, and you will have something that everybody has been thinking about. Of course, if nothing special suggests itself, a topic from some topic book may be shown, but I never would follow any topic simply because it was in the book.

Another thing, do not be too formal nor too exhaustive in your opening remarks, or you will get more than you aim for. I do not say that a man should only talk so long. That depends—ten minutes may be too short or too long, according to circumstances. His opening should be like a lever to turn on the power, and if a foot will do, all right. Some places need more than others, but be sure you have something for somebody else. One reason I never can get any help out of these books on Bible readings, etc., is because they help too much. I have read so hard to keep up with them that I haven't any strength left to go alone and then try to keep the people reasonably close to the topic. If the Lord puts a thought into a man's heart or a song into a man's heart it ought to come out, and I venture to affirm that it will, if the Lord puts it there, have some relation to the topic, if that is also from the Lord. But my trouble is, I announced a topic and nobody for some time seemed inclined to respect it or to talk upon it, but a few kind words and a great deal of perseverance have accomplished much. And further, remember to encourage all to come to prayer. I say encourage, because no one wishes to come to anything as a criminal. Encourage the business men; take them individually; show them how they need it, how their Christian strength will be increased; how their souls will obtain rest, and do this especially if you live in a city where it is the fashion to seek rest anywhere but in God's house. What sight more effective than to see a young man and his employer in the same prayer-room? And finally, look out for the working of the spirit in every meeting; you expect it in some way, not in all.

Dr. Lawrence, through Mr. Moody, asked Mr. Sankey, before leaving, to sing hymn 378, "Beyond the Smiling and the Weeping," one, the people were reminded by Mr. Moody, that was held a favorite by President Garfield. So the song was tenderly sung, Mr. Sankey being assisted in the refrain by a lady's voice that proved a very tuneful coadjutor.

Mr. Charles M. Morton, pastor of Railroad Chapel, then, as the assigned ten-minute speaker on the above topic, advanced, and began by saying that it was the world's verdict that prayer meetings were not interesting. Whenever they were interesting it was the exception. The world had only grace enough to enjoy that which was interesting. There was a grand little band in every prayer meeting ready to bear their part in whatever came up. In most prayer meetings we knew every one who was going to pray, and what they were going to pray about.

The only question was as to how long they would pray. He had been in such prayer meetings, and he thanked the Lord that he did not live in the town, so that he would have to attend such meetings all the time.

In every prayer meeting there were men and women capable of doing good work. But something must happen to break the ice and bring these to the surface. The men who sprang to the surface soon after being converted were the men who did the best work. John B. Gough said he had as much diffidence now in appearing before an audience as he did when he first began work in the lecture field. But when he began to speak he was all the better for his diffidence.

Mr. Morton then gave his own experience in being converted under the preaching of Moody.

The leader of the meeting should have a great deal of common sense. Common sense and the Holy Spirit in such places were generally found together. The leader should only make suggestions, so that the others might take them up. But too often the leader talked for half an hour, exhausting the subject, and leave nothing for others to say. He had seen leaders in the noon meetings in Farwell Hall talk for thirty-five minutes, and then sit down and ask the brethren to be brief. He thought that to do that required a good deal of cheek. It was just like when he was a boy and had to wait when there was company. He was posted at the door to see if there was anything left for the children, and he generally found that there was not much. The leaders used up all that was good and left only the chaff and middlings for any who followed him.

Then there should be care in the selection of hymns to be sung. These were too often wholly out of order in the meeting. There were some hymns, he thought, that were mere stuff anyway, and fit for no meeting. For instance, "Plunged in a gulf of dark despair." There was no comfort or enjoyment in singing such hymns.

The prayers should be short and for each other rather than for something they knew nothing about. It did a man a great deal of good to hear himself or his friends prayed for. It made him feel that his friends thought of him.

The next topic and speaker were

"METHODS OF ORGANIZATION FOR RELIGIOUS WORK."

Mr. William Reynolds, of Peoria, Illinois, spoke as follows on this subject:

He supposed that there were hundreds of people in the audience whose pleasure had been somewhat marred because there had not been present others whom they would have liked to have had their own enjoyment of this great feast. He supposed that there were possibly hundreds of ministers, who as they had been sitting in the meeting during the session of the convention, had been longing and wishing that the people could be with them to hear all the things that had been said and enjoyed.

He would not attempt to theorize. What he would have to say would be of a very practical character, and everything that he should advocate would be things that he had tried and found to succeed. If he was to take a text for his remarks he would take two, as follows: "Go, son, work in my vineyard," and "To every man his work."

God never said work to any one excepting to His children, to those to whom He had given the power of becoming sons of God. God expected service from none but His children. The speaker thanked God that there was as much Christian activity in the churches as there existed to-day. There never had been in the history of the world so much Christian effort as now, as there was at this hour. In this State of Illinois alone there were 60,000 men and women teaching God's word in the Sabbath school. In this Union there were 750,000 of its best men and women teaching voluntarily, without money or price, God's word. But only a fragment of the church were doing its work.

What could be done to develop workers out of the idle element of the church? We had the talent, the men and women, the brain and heart of the country, and the world inside the church, that we might use and that would be willing to be used, if they knew what to do, if properly pursued. How could we make them realize their responsibility and stir them up to do their duty, or what it is rather their privilege to do, for it ought to be a privilege to work for Him who died for us—saved us by His blood.

As a result of the convention, the speaker expected that better sermons would be preached next Sunday throughout all the Northwest than had been preached for three years, perhaps for five years past, and he thought the theme of them would be what the preachers had seen at the convention. He advised every minister to tell what he had seen. They should not let the melted ore cool, but go to work at once when they had stirred up their congregation, and mould their people into workers. Many failed to do this. That was the trouble. They were stirred up by a good stimulative sermon, but let its effect cool till its influence was lost. What was wanted was organization. They had been told the day before that it was the best organized political party that won in a campaign. The best organized army won the battle. Many of our churches were said to be like great religious mobs. They came together and went away; and nothing was accomplished.

Wesley and Whitfield were mighty men in the last century. What was the result of their work? Where now were the results of Whitfield's works? Largely in heaven, sitting at the right hand of God.

What did Wesley leave? Not so great a man as Whitfield, but what was the result of his work? The grandest church in this country. Why was there this difference between the results of the work of these two men? The difference lay between Wesley's organized work and Whitfield's work without organization. We must put every man into his adapted place of work; not try to make every man do the same kind of work. Some men are fitted for one thing, some for another, and if put into the wrong place will be sure to fail.

If a man was found not to succeed in one place he should be put into another, and another, until the right place was found for him.

The speaker knew a man once. He had a big heart, a broad face, and still a broader smile, but he had a most wonderful faculty of getting rid of his Sunday-school class [Laughter] that he had ever heard of. Now that man has found a place in the church that just suited his talents. He was placed at the door to receive the people as they came in, and the broad smile and the hearty manner and his big heart made him a grand success.

He was a man of grace in that church, because people with such welcomes as he gave them were made to feel at home in the church, and they came again. There must be division of church work, and it must be organized work in every division. If the speaker was looking for a minister he would look for a good organizer in preference to a good pulpit orator, not that he did not think highly of the latter, but because organizing powers would do more than oratorical powers.

Every element in the church should be organized. They should be organized into three divisions, to be sub-divided if necessary. The first division should be the Sunday-school, for that was the right arm of the church. The next division should have charge of the missionary work—going out visiting from house to house. That was next in importance.

The third should be the social department. Some were specially adapted to this work, though good for nothing as Sunday-school teachers or as missionaries. This department was an important one, because the social element in our Nation was an important part of it and should be administered to. A good sanctified laugh was a good thing. If the church wanted to keep the young men and young women in the church, it must look well after this department. The social element must be recognized.

Next, it should be understood that any one who joins the church joins with the expectation of going to work, and something suitable to them must be given them to do. The school children must be turned into teachers. A young home visitor must be sent with an old one to learn the best methods.

At the close of Mr. Reynold's remarks a duet was sung by Mr. and Mrs. McGranahan, and afterward Hymn 102 by the congregation.

The hour, 4:30, being then arrived for the opening of the "Question Drawer," Mr. Moody bent himself to the answering of queries.

THE QUESTION DRAWER.

The first question was:

"Is not an association for women as much needed as that for the men in Christian work?"

What I have seen of these associations in this country and Europe, I have found they have much that is good. These associations reach the girls in the city and save them from ruin. When in Liverpool I visited a building which was being erected there for such an association by the women of England. It is as fine a building as in the city, and the ladies have built it without the assistance of the men. It will be opened next month. In the several rooms in that building the girls of the city who go there to get work will be instructed in the Bible and made good Christian women. They are not only taught on the Sabbath but during evenings through the week. We talk about the expense of such institutions. Why, nothing will stop expense but death, and a man who is afraid of expense had better die. I was glad of the opportunity to go to a man the other day and ask him for $50,000. He said he had not given $50,000 in a lump for a good while, and he hesitated. But he said he had made it a rule to give $500 a day to some good work, and he never went to bed at night until this had been accomplished. I say, Lord bless such men. We need just such men.

There are lots of men in this country who would be much happier if they would give $500 a day for a year or two to some good cause. It is estimated that there are 30,000 fallen women in the city of Chicago. I hope that is not so, but if it is there is a great opportunity for work here. Remember that it is not themselves alone, but they are dragging down your sons to degradation. If there was a Woman's Christian Association here to help these women and prevent them from going so low it would be a great work. But Dr. Lorimer knows more about it than I do, let us hear from him.

Dr. Lorimer said he was always ready to lend a hand in Mr. Moody's work. Talk about the expense of such institutions as this referred to, the people should see that it was the wisest economy to prevent crime. There was a Woman's Christian Association in Chicago, but it had no building of its own as it should. And the ladies of Chicago should be ashamed that it did not. There were ladies of wealth here and a building could be erected without trouble. We were talking too much about women's rights. He would not say but he was in favor of the women having their rights. He was a great defender of the purity of women. It would make the heart sick to show what were the scant earnings of the girls who come to this great city and found work. They were so scant that one was surprised to know that any people had to clothe themselves and live respectable on the allowance. And that was one reason why they did not live respectable. They did not go into such lives because they liked it; they were more often driven to it. The city should have an association to look after these. In this great city it was a shame that so little was being done for the purity of women. In Boston and New York there were associations with large buildings. The doctor hoped that something practical would come of this convention, and nothing better could be done than this kind of work. The Christian people wanted to impress upon the world that they were interested in fallen humanity.

Mr. Moody said one thing had impressed him in the old country, and that was the number of institutions there. There were so many, too, that were carried on by men and women privately. In Scotland and England there were hundreds of missions and chapels and homes and other like institutions supported by private individuals. In Edinburgh one lady had a child hospital, and she not only paid for its support but she visited it daily and helped nurse the little people.

"Are we going to get money for all these missions?"

I heard a man complaining yesterday that he had not been called to give anything for a long time. I have no doubt that we will get all the money needed. I would just as soon go and ask a man for $50,000 as not. You are not asking for money for yourself, remember. It is for the Lord, and you can ask for it with perfect good grace.

"Is it best to have one speaker or two at an evangelistic meeting?"

One, by all means. I have often seen one man get up and make a good impression, and another come along and wipe it out. It is better, too, to have one man right along for several weeks. And I want to say right here—not to flatter you—that Chicago has to-day better and abler ministers than I ever knew before in my twenty-seven years' knowledge of the place. I never saw the churches so well manned. Let us thank God for such men. No city in the country has so much ability in her pulpits to-day as Chicago. If these men were invited into the different parts of the city they would draw crowded houses and do great good. They would not, of course, care to go to preach to empty benches, and I don't blame them for refusing to go to preach where preparation has not been made for good meetings. The greatest work that had been done in England had been in missions established by the Church of England. The different churches in the great cities had established these missions and their different ministers left their own pulpits for ten days and gave this time to the missions. Some of them went from one mission to another and gave up several weeks to this work. The preachers of Chicago could be induced to do the same, and such men as Dr. Lorimer and Dr. Hatfield would fill the churches and convert many people.

Let the pastors on the North Side, and the South Side and the West Side change pulpits, and hold revivals. There was no danger but that the people would come out to hear such men, if the speakers were well advertised. Some ministers objected to having their names placarded on the walls, but why should they?

The theatres advertised their plays, and why should not the churches advertise their work. There would be no trouble in always getting the people if a little common sense was used. There were a hundred men in Chicago who could preach the gospel better than any of the evangelists from abroad. Mr. Moody did not think that one or two sermons a week would convert Chicago. There must be sermons every day. He then told the story of his own conversion, and said he attended services in Boston for weeks, and every Sunday he felt thrilled by what he heard from the pulpit, but before another sermon came the effect of the last had been lost. Had there been sermons every day he would have been converted much sooner. It was practical to convert Chicago. It was a good place to start this new movement in. The men who could preach should do nothing else. They should let all the machinery of the church go and do nothing but preach. There were men who had talents for different parts of the work. Some were good pastors and some were capable of looking after the machinery, and others were good preachers. Some of the preachers were afraid of repeating themselves. He was not. He believed in repeating a good thing. When a man preached a sermon that moved the people and had good results, he should repeat it to others and see if he could not convert them. In England good sermons were repeated, and he remembered one place where he saw it announced as the 485th night of one service. When he found that he had a sermon that the people liked he would not take the trouble to get up another until that had been exhausted. Those who wanted a new sermon every day, and were afraid of repeating themselves, were afraid of losing their dignity. They wanted to maintain their reputation for learning.

"Can you tell us anything about the Mildmay?"

I wish we had a Mildmay in this town. The Church of England started it several years ago. There are training-schools there where people are trained for different works. There was a training school for nurses, and these nurses were sent for all over the country. They were Christian women, and by their influence as nurses were able to do a great deal for Christianity.

Chicago was a good place for this work.

"Is a person justified all at once?"

Yes. But sanctification is another thing.

"How do you get children interested in sermons?"

At my school in Northfield I wanted my boys to hear Mr. Pentecost preach, and, as it was late, I was afraid they would go to sleep. So to keep them awake I offered to give the boy one dollar who could remember most of what he said. The result was they all got note books and pencils and began writing down what he said. Some of them remembered nearly everything he said. Some ministers give up five minutes of their sermon to the children. They need not fear spoiling the sermon. To get hold of the parents the best way is to get the children.

"Is it well to number converts?."

Elijah got into trouble by trying to number Israel. It is best to let the Lord keep the record. It makes me creep all over to hear a man tell how many he has converted. It is best not to triumph.

"Is there any danger starting men into the work too young?"

There is a good deal of danger, in not starting them to work soon enough. Pitt was in Parliament at 21 and was Prime Minister at 22. Napoleon was young and Alexander had conquered the world at 32. There is danger sometimes in flattering young men who are at work for Christ. Spiritual pride is a very great injury. The young men in Chicago could be used to good advantage. They could go out and talk seven nights in the week while the minister preached but one. And these young men could reach men who could not be approached by anybody else.

"Do you believe in open air preaching."

Yes; but not every man who can talk is fit to preach to open-air audiences. It needs a peculiar talent to go there. He wants to have tact, to know how to get along with these people. These meetings were attended by shrewd men, infidels and skeptics, and they were always ready to trip up the preacher. The man preaching to open-air audiences should not allow himself to be drawn into controversy.

"How can you get the people out to the week day meetings?"

Make them interesting. The prayer-meeting should be made interesting. The great work of the church was in the prayer-meeting. Make the prayer meetings short and pithy. Send the people away hungry that will want to come again. I knew a man once who preached until he had driven every soul away from the church. He said he thought it was a pity to stop as long as he had any body to preach to.

"What do you mean by a training school?"

A place where men well along in life could go and study and receive training for religious work. They are too old to go off to school. They need to be prepared for the work and they have not the time to take a regular course at the colleges and the seminary. They are to be taught in the Bible. In this work of saving souls we want the laymen as well as the preachers. There are hundreds of young men in Chicago who would go into such schools and be fitted for the work. We want to train the women too. In Northfield we have a ladies' seminary, and the girls are educated for this work. They are the ones to go to the fallen women. The men have no business in such places. It is the women, the great-hearted, noble women, who can save their fallen sisters. A lady in Birmingham has devoted herself to this work, and has rescued over 300 women. It is sad that Chicago, with its 30,000 fallen women cannot be reached and saved. Then men should be taught in German and French. I would give $100,000, if I had it, could I speak German. There is a great work to be done there, and the doors are open. There is no reason why there should not be another such a revival there as that started by Martin Luther.

There were other questions, but Mr. Moody had already used up more than his half hour, and the audience was beginning to tire of the long session. The long meter doxology was sung, and the people dismissed.

EVENING SESSION.

The feature of this evening service was

MR. MOODY'S SERMON.

His text was found in Titus ii, 11, 12, 13 and 14. "For the grace of God that bringeth salvation hath appeared to all men.

"Teaching us, denying ungodliness and worldly lusts, we should live soberly, righteously, and godly in this present world;

"Looking for that blessed hope and the glorious appearance of the great God and our Savior, Jesus Christ;

"Who gave Himself for us, that He might redeem us from all iniquity and purify unto Himself a peculiar people, zealous of good works."

Mr. Moody spoke as follows:

I want to call your attention to grace in a three-fold aspect: Grace that bringeth salvation; and grace for living, grace for service; the grace of God that bringeth salvation as it appears to all men. He didn't send it, but Christ came and brought salvation, and Christ is God's gift to this world. He gave Him up freely for us all; and if a man is lost it is because he spurns God's gift, because he won't take Christ as his Savior.

Now, salvation is as free as the air we breathe. I believe that in Christendom where the gospel is preached, more men are kept out of the kingdom of God because they are trying to merit salvation by their works and their own virtue than any other one thing. Now it is "To him that worketh not, but believeth." I will admit salvation is worth going around this world on our hands and knees for it, it is worth climbing its mountains, swimming its rivers, and going through its deserts—but we are not going to get salvation in that way, but we must take it on God's terms, and that is as a gift. We work because we are saved—not to be saved. When we work to be saved we work away from the cross and not toward it. After salvation is ours we are ready to work. A good many men are trying to work to heaven, and throw this passage into your face:

"Work out your salvation with fear and trembling."

How are you going to work out what you have not got? Suppose you send your boy to school and tell him he may spend $500, but he has not got it to spend—how can he spend it? I gave my boy this year a part of the garden to plant with just what he pleased. I said:

"I will give it to you on condition that you work it out and don't let the weeds get the advantage of you," and he took it and went to work. Now, he had to have it before he could work it.

You might as well try to leap over the moon as to work out your salvation in your own name and strength. You can't do it. It is the gift of God, and Paul says in Ephesians, first chapter and second verse:

"For by grace ye are saved. By grace and not by yourselves; for that is the gift of God. Take heed lest ye should boast."

There is a good deal of boasting in Chicago, but you will hear nothing of that in Heaven. Men get suddenly rich here, and they will tell you how they came here poor boys and got rich, and they are very proud of the money they have accumulated. But when you come into the kingdom of God, all boasting is excluded. We have got to come as a beggar. Some one has said that if you come to God as a beggar you will go away as a prince, and if you come to Him as a prince you will go away as a beggar. Now, there is no apostle who has said so much about works for salvation and about salvation as Paul.

A man ought to work day and night if he is saved; he ought not have a lazy hair in his head or a lazy drop of blood in his veins. What had Saul ever done up to the time Christ met him? He had done everything that he could to stamp out Christianity. He was then in the very act of going to Damascus to take every one he could find that called upon Jesus, and bind them and kill them;

but Christ met him, and He dealt in Grace with him. The voice that he heard out of Heaven was the voice of love:

"Saul, Saul, why persecutest thou Me?"

And the hard heart of Saul was broken, and he was ready to receive the crucified Christ, and instead of going to crucify Christ, he went to praise and glorify God. I was in a Southern city awhile ago, and a minister pointed out in the congregation a man, and told me his history. When the war broke out he lived on the other side of Mason and Dixon line, and of course, he joined the Southern army. He was arrested as a spy, and was tried by court-martial and was condemned to be shot. In the cell, waiting to be executed, every time the soldiers took in his rations—it seemed as if he laid awake nights to heap up names against Abraham Lincoln. It made the soldiers angry; and at last they got so mad they said they would be glad when the bullet went through his heart.

They would like to have silenced that tongue, and they wanted to let him starve to death. One day an officer came to the man. He was still full of bitterness, and he expected the officer had come to order him out to be shot. When the officer came in he commenced again against Abraham Lincoln, but the officer handed him a pardon, signed by the President of the United States, Abraham Lincoln. The man looked at the pardon, and then broke down and wept like a child. He said: "Abraham Lincoln pardoned me, that never spoke a good word for him." The officer said:

"You have some good friend in Washington, and he has got Mr. Lincoln to pardon you."

And the minister said:

"There is no man in the country that is more reverent to the memory of Lincoln than that man."

That is grace. There is not a man in Chicago that salvation is not offered to, "Whosoever will, let him come and partake of the water of life freely." And do you know that is the last invitation let down into this thirsty world. I can imagine after Paul had written his letter that the Master Eye could see that somebody would be stumbling over the doctrine of election, and would be in despair because they were not of the elect. John was in the spirit on the Lord's day in Patmos—and what a day that must have been for John when he heard that old familiar voice. For sixty years he had not heard it, and when that gentle hand was again laid upon him how it must have thrilled him.

And he heard that sweet, silver Voice saying:

"John, write these things to the church!" And he took up his pen and wrote. And the Voice said: "Put in one more invitation before you seal up the book!" And this is the last invitation let down into this world: "The Spirit and the bride say, Come. Let him that heareth come." And he wrote, and the Voice again said: "Put this in, 'Whosoever will, let him come and take of the water of life freely." Friend, will you take it to-night? It is freely offered. I read some time ago of a Sunday school teacher who had a class of little boys, and he had a silver watch, and he offered it to the largest boy in the class, and says: "Take that watch; I give it to you." And the little boy laughed at him and wouldn't take it. And he offered it to the next one, and the next one, and when he got to the smallest boy in the class the little fellow reached up and took it. [Laughter.] The teacher said: "Keep it and put it in your pocket, you have taken me at my word. Take it home. It is yours. Don't bring it back to me." And the rest of the class says: "Teacher, you didn't mean that. You didn't mean to give him that for good?"

"Yes, I did," said the teacher.

"Oh! if we had known that, we would have taken it.". (Laughter.)

You would not have to go out of Chicago or out of Farwell Hall to-night to see that boy. When we speak to you about this unspeakable gift, there is not a man in this hall that would turn from it if he thought the gift was in his reach.

Now let me pass to the second head: "Grace for living," teaching us, denying ungodly lusts, etc. Now, dear friends, I believe a good many people get the gift without getting light. They don't get it in all its benefits. He came that we might have life more freely and more abundantly, and I believe that there are hundreds and thousands of our church members who are like Lazarus when he came out of the sepulchre. They are bound hand and foot, with a napkin around their mouth—they can't speak. They are without power to use their tongues. Jesus came that we might have grace in all its fullness, and that we might have life abundantly, and if we have not got it there is no one to blame but ourselves. He says: "Boldly come out and get help in the time of need." Is it not the time of need now? Do you mothers not need grace to train your children for time and eternity?. Don't you laymen need God to direct you in your business? O, I pray most fervently that the low standard in the church of God may be raised. If we could only get the standard higher and get filled with the grace of God we would see marvelous results. I do not fear the opposition outside of the church one-half that I fear the low standard in the church.

I fear the casting of shadows around the heart of the word of God a thousand times more than the Roman spear that went to His heart These so-called friends of the cross, and yet its enemies, by their worldly lives! They have the name, but not the power.

"Teaching us, denying ungodliness in every shape." He died for that very purpose—that he might redeem us from all iniquity, and I do pray earnestly that this convention may result in a higher standard of Christian life right here in Chicago. I said to my friend, Mr. Sankey: "I don't know but we might better go up and preach to Christendom, and go right through the church, and preach to you Christ and His grace than to sinners." Whenever you have seen the church setting its face toward Bethel, and coming out of Shechem, and out of Egypt and coming up to Bethel, the power of God seems to fall upon the ungodly, and the churches are crowded with men inquiring the way to Zion. What we want is more grace. If you ask me what the church of God needs more than any other thing, I would say *grace*, that we might live to adorn the doctrine of Jesus Christ.

Now, you find a great many people in bondage and in constant fear. They are in fear that death is going to be dark and terrible, and things before them are dark and gloomy.

Dr. Bonner made this remark some time ago, that gave me a great lift. Once in a while a sentence from a child of God will be like a flood of light. He made the statement that "There is nothing before the true believer that is not glorious." If we get that into our minds we would not be so sad, cast down and gloomy. And if you will show me a church that is full of joy and gladness I will show you a church that God has used. And if we can only realize that everything before us is glorious, we would be of good cheer, and we would sing songs of gladness. I went to my Bible and I found our garments are to be grace and glory, our songs are to be songs of glory, our home is to be the home of the glorified, and our rest is to be glory. This vile body is to be fashioned as His glorious body. "Ah," some of you say, "Death!" Well, death is only the gateway of immortality. It is through the portals of death that we pass into everlasting life. All that death can do to the true believer is to take down the house and put him into a far better one; a body that cannot be tainted by sin; a body like His own. Speaking about death, I think that the twenty-third Psalm is more misquoted than any other one thing in the whole Bible.

How many times I have heard people get up in our social prayer meetings and quote the verse in that psalm:

"Yea, though I walk through the dark valley"—and then emphasize "dark." Do you know *dark* is not in it. It says: "Yea, though I walk through the valley of the shadow." Did you ever see a shadow where there was not light? Put out the light in this hall; go down into a cellar, and see if there is a shadow. All that death can do is to throw its shadow across our path. Well, a shadow don't hurt us. We can walk right through a shadow.

Dear friends, what we want is to live in the power of the gospel, and we haven't a thing to fear in life or in death. If we could get more of the grace of God, that shall lift us up above all these circumstances. People say: "Well, you don't know the difficulties and trials I have. You don't know the circumstances that surround me." Well, my friends, what does the psalm say? "As thy day is, so shall thy strength be. My grace is sufficient for thee." And if He had grace enough to carry the twelve apostles in such a triumphant way at the end, has He not grace to carry us to the end. Talk about our sufferings! What are our sufferings to the sufferings of the early church?

I don't know but that if the sufferings of martyrdom were to come again it would be better for the church of God. It would burn out this luke-warm spirit that is with us. In the second century a king told a martyr that if he didn't recant from his Christian belief he would banish him, and he said: "Oh, king, you can't banish me from Christ, because I am with Him to the end of time." The king said: "I will take your property away." He said: "My treasures are upon high and you can't get at them." The king stamped his foot on the ground, and shouted: "I will kill you." And he says: "You can't; I have been dead forty years in Christ." What can you do with such martyrs as that? Let the king take his life; he would only be in glory in the presence of the King.

Now I come to the third head. There is grace enough if we will only eat what bread God gives us. He died that He might redeem us and make us a peculiar people, jealous of good works. I hope the people of this convention will be stirred up to good works. If we can only light up our torch and go to our different fields of labor, this convention will do us more good than any convention ever held in the Northwest.

Here are representatives of the whole Northwest, and God can use the weakest saint here, if you are only willing to be used. Some one sent me a tract entitled, "What is That in Thy Hand?" I liked the title, and it brings out this thought: When God called Moses to go down into Egypt, Moses began to excuse himself. At last God said, "What is that in thy hand?" It was a rod which Moses had cut from a bramble bush, probably to help him tend his sheep. And God said: "With that, ye shall deliver the children of Israel." I can imagine Moses starting down into Egypt and meeting some freethinker who had been acquainted with him. He said to Moses:

"Moses, where are you going?"
"I am going down to Egypt."
"What are you going down there for?"

"To bring up three million of bondmen."
"Do you think Pharaoh will let them go?"
"I don't know. I will bring them."
"Where is your army?"
"I have no army."
"What will you do it with?"
"With this rod."

Why, he would have thought the man was clean crazy, but bear in mind God had linked His almighty power to that rod. He had given His word that Moses should deliver the children of Israel. I suppose the king looked upon the rod with a great deal of contempt, but when he refused to let the children of Israel go, Moses turned the waters into blood with it, and he brought plague upon the Egyptians with it, and when he stretched that rod out over the waters of the Red Sea, the mighty host of God passed through dry shod. When they wanted water in the wilderness He struck the rock with that rod and a pure, beautiful stream flowed out, and the weary, thirsty multitude were revived by it. Centuries have rolled away but the story of the rod has not failed yet. Let us give God what we have, and not what we have not got. You say you haven't much. Just use what you have got. A man said some time ago that he felt like a mere cipher. Just put God alongside of a cipher and it becomes a good deal. When a man is next to nobody God will take him up and use him.

When the committee of official men from Jerusalem went down to see who John the Baptist was, he said: "I am nobody. I am nothing but a voice." But when Christ came John began to preach down himself and up Christ, and he was a mighty preacher. When we, who are nothing, want to work for Christ, He will use us. Look at Joshua with his 600,000 men walking around the walls of Jericho. Suppose you had met him on the seventh day and asked him:

"Joshua, what does all this performance mean. You have been walking around here six days. What are you going to do?"

"I am going to take the walls of Jericho."

"You are?"

"Yes; we will have them down before night."

"Where is your battery? Where is your artillery?"

"Here with these rams' horns."

And they went on blowing their rams' horns and down went the walls of Jericho. If we cannot blow a fine trumpet let us take what we have, and with a stammering tongue, but with a heart on fire for God, we can be used.

Take Gideon. When he marshaled his 32,000 men, and he knew the Midianites had 130,000 men, his heart sank within him, and he said:

"What shall I do with these 30,000 men?"

But the Lord said: "You have got too many. Take those that are afraid and send them home to their mothers. Take two-thirds of this audience of this house and let them go away, and if the rest of us have God with us we will be more than equal to the whole number. Gideon had only 10,000 men left, but the Lord said: "Gideon, you have got too many yet, take them down to the brook and try them." And all but 300 rushed down to the brook, and the Lord says:

"Those 300 men are the men whose hearts will be loyal to the king. Let us have them."

The first Quaker said that every Quaker ought to shake the country for miles around him. Wesley said if he had a hundred men that feared nothing but sin he would set up the gates of God on earth, and I believe he would. If you had met Gideon with his 300 men you would have said:

"Where are you going?"

"Going out to meet those Midianites."

"What have you got to meet them with?"

"Some pitchers and some lights in them."

What a contemptible thing, you would think. But Gideon went on and routed the Midianites with just those empty pitchers. He used what he had.

Take Samson. He was going out to fight a thousand men. Suppose you had met him and said:

"Why, Samson, what have you got to meet those men with?"

"The jaw-bone of an ass."

I suppose he just saw it on the ground and picked it up, and the Lord helped him and he slew a thousand men. Now if the Lord can use the jaw-bone of an ass, can He not use you? Will you let Him use you? I heard a man in Scotland say that every man in Saul's army knew that God could use him to meet Goliath, but there was only one man that knew He would, and went out and slew Goliath.

There is a good deal of difference between what God can do and what God will do. I believe every one here thinks God can use him, but how many would take five stones out of the brook and go out and meet the giant.

Samson was playing with a shamgard, I heard a preacher in Glasgow say, and a man came running over the hill and said: "Six thousand Philistines are coming after you." Samson said: "I can take care of them." And he took his oxgoad and slew 400 of them. He used what he had.

The Bible is full of such instances. Look at the man out there in the desert with but five little barley loaves and two small fishes.

I can imagine how the disciples, when they were giving bread to the first man, gave him a very small bit, but it held out, and by and by they gave larger pieces, and soon they were breaking the loaves in two, and giving every man all he wanted. Look at that good Samaritan. Look into his saddle-bags, and you will find that he had but a little oil, but it was a pretty good thing for the man that fell among thieves. Some people would have wanted to save him with sermons, but you have got to have something else. That Samaritan preached a grand sermon, when he poured the oil into his wounds. Suppose he had brought out a large manuscript or a long article on science. The poor man didn't want that, he wanted some one to care for him, and get his arm under him and lift him up.

Many a man in Chicago has fallen among thieves and among drunkards and among harlots, and he wants some one to tell him not what a bad man he is, but to come to him in pity and try to help him out. Some people carry a bottle of vinegar, but it is better to have oil. Sometimes I think it is better to get above this sectarian feeling. You know the Jews hated no people worse than Samaritans. They wouldn't sell them anything. You know a Jew has to hate a man pretty well if he wont sell to him. The Jews believed that the Samaritans hadn't even a soul. In this parable of the Good Samaritan God teaches us to rise above this miserable sectarian feeling—shall we stop and ask whether a man is a Roman Catholic or a Protestant?

If we see a man perishing let us hasten to his help, and use what we have got. Dorcas used only a little needle, but how she set the needle going through the earth. Mary had an alabaster box of ointment. It was not worth much, I suppose, but she dropped it upon the feet of the Saviour, and the fragrance of it is in the church to-day.

"I do not know that Mary was a strong-minded woman, or that she was wealthy as beautiful; perhaps she did not move in the very best society, but there is one thing I do know—she could love. Wherever the gospel of the Son of God is preached, that story is told out. I suppose Mary forgot all about herself, but she loved the Master, and she poured that ointment out upon Him. Eighteen centuries have rolled away, but the name of Mary of Bethany is as fresh as it ever was. I suppose there is no woman's name so fresh as her's, except the name of Mary, the mother of the Savior. I can imagine some man when Christ was on earth, prophesying that that story would be told in the nineteenth century, and not a man on the face of the earth would have believed it. We look back on the days of miracles, but we forget we are living in the days of miracles. Missionary societies in New York and London have put the story of Mary into 250 languages, and have sent out millions of copies of it. That story will live as long as the Church of God is upon earth. She made herself immortal by that one act. Nothing you do for Jesus Christ is small. We want to-day men and women who are willing to do.

I suppose if these reporters had been living in the days of Mary, and heard on the streets of Jerusalem that she had broken that alabaster box upon Him, they would not have thought it was worth noticing; but it has outlived everything else that took place then. If they had seen that widow cast those two mites into the treasury of the Lord they would have said, "There will be no one in Jerusalem that will care for that."

But see! Eighteen centuries have rolled away, and that story has outlived anything else that occurred there.

If a man gave a thousand pounds to the temple the Jerusalem reporters would have published that in their papers. [Laughter.] When the widow cast in her mite, the Lord saw her act, and He said:

"She has given more than all of them."

If there is heart in it, God will accept your service. If you have only one talent, and make use of that, you will hear the Master say in the evening of life, "Well done." We should never call anything small that we do for the Lord. When the prophet's servant came back and said he saw a little cloud no larger than a man's hand coming up out of the sea Elijah knew what that meant, and he said:

"Make haste and tell Ahab to get home."

He knew there was abundance of rain in that cloud. Have you a Sunday school class? It is a great thing to be permitted to be a co-worker with God. It is a great thing to have the privilege of leading one little ewe lamb into the kingdom of God.

I remember of being in a place some time ago, and I saw a teacher who had a class at 3 o'clock. I said:

"Have you a class at 3 o'clock?"

"Oh!" she says, "I have a class."

"Were you at your class to-day?"

"No, sir."

"Did you tell the Superintendent you would not be there?"

"No, Sir."

"Did you get a substitute?"

"No, sir."

"Well," I said, "did your class have any teacher to-day?"

"I think not, for I saw a good many teachers in the hall to hear you."

"Who took her room?"

"I suppose no one did."

"Is that the way you take to do the Lord's work?"

"Well, you see, there are only five persons in the class?"

Now, among that five persons, I said, there may be one who might be a reformation in himself—a Wesley, a Whitfield, a Luther, a Melancthon. It is a great thing to have five human souls to teach. Each one of this class may become a herald from heaven, a blessing from above, and do a hundred times more good than you can do. And each man and woman can well afford to spend a whole life to get even one soul into the kingdom of God. Paul, who brought Simon and Peter to Christ. And what did they? Peter got three thousand at one time. Peter led them to Christ. And, dear friends, you may be instrumentalities in leading some one of these thousands of foreigners to Christ, and they may go back to their older country and be themselves the instruments of lighting up their own people with the glory of God, and spreading around the glad tidings of Christ. Oh, that God might take the scales from over our eyes to-night that we might have the glorious luxury of working for Him to-night.

I believe that there is not an angel in heaven but what would, if they could have the privilege of leading one soul to God, would come down to earth to do it.

It is a great privilege, a wonderful privilege, to be the instrumentality in the hands of God of leading one dear, precious soul to God. Now, my dear friends shall we not at this hour come again fresh to God? We ourselves cannot convert the world. Our world is not responsible to us. We must simply be faithful. God will judge our work and reward us for it. I believe that if the archangel Gabriel himself should come down to-night and should preach with all the eloquence of heaven itself and every offer should be held up to his hearers, with the glory of that upper world painted before them, there would not be a soul among them converted excepting through the Holy Ghost working upon it. All we have got to do, dear friends, is to preach Christ crucified and tell the story of the cross, and the Lord will do the rest. He will bless the seed we sow.

Let us sow it by the side of the living waters. A word spoken here and a word spoken there will be blessed of God and souls will be gathered up. The converting is for the Lord. The thanks should be to the Lord. Oh that we may all be anointed afresh to-night, and that many hearts may be kindled afresh.

I see a man sitting over there whom I know, and I hope he will go back home to preach with renewed strength from God. I see men from distant portions of the West—men from St. Louis. I hope that God will send them, too, to work still better than they have worked before. Perhaps it is only for a little while, a few days, a few weeks, a few months, that they will have to work in, and then all their chance for work will be over. If we are going to wipe away the bitter tears from the helpless widow's eye, if we are going to lend relief to that poor, fatherless child, let us make haste. The day will soon be ended, the night will soon be here. There is no time to waste. I remember that when I was in Liverpool I made this promise: I said to a lady if you will find four likely boys, I will try to have them trained at Northfield. I came home. Only a few weeks had passed away. I was ready to retire to bed at 10:30 at night, when I heard the ring of the telephone, and I sent to my office, and the station men telephoned up to me that there were three boys wanting me. I telephoned back to have them sent to a hotel till morning, and when I went there the next morning I found three brothers that were orphans. Then I remembered my promise. When I made that remark in Liverpool I forgot all about it in a few minutes after making it. Even then the mother of these three boys was dying.

I did not know it, but God knew if I did not. Their father had been a hard-working man—a solicitor. He had died and left her a widow with three children—three boys. They came over to me well dressed. You could see from their appearance that a devoted, loving mother had lavished her affection upon them—had cared for them with a true mother's love. Her boys told me of that mother's grief on her dying bed that she had to leave them, with no one to care for them. Their mother was now in the grave far away. I felt when these three boys came to me that I had had given to me a great privilege—the privilege of having those orphans sent to me, a gift from God. It refreshed my soul to think that I could look at them, after the promise I had made at Liverpool. It was only a word—a single remark—that dropped from their lips, but the fruit of it came back to me, and the three are now in one room. They have got the photographs with them of their loving mother. Think of it, how it all happened She died, and the next week they were on their way over the sea to their new home, and now we are educating and training them, hoping that when prepared they may go out to foreign lands as missionaries to spread abroad the gospel of God Oh, what a blessed privilege it is to have the privilege of working for Christ; to have the privilege of doing a little—ever so little. My friends, if you do not know what to do go to some one older, some one more experienced than yourselves, and find out from them what you can best do.

If I had a thousand working bodies instead of one, I could find work for each to do. I remember how I did when I first tried to work for the Lord. I did not know much. I did not know which way to turn; what was the best thing I could do. But I did something. I did my little work the best way I could. And then God blessed me, and kept giving me more and more to do, until I got so much to do that if I had had a thousand different bodies to work with I would still have had enough to do. Now, dear friends, if any of you cannot hold as high a position as you would wish and desire to hold, take such a position as you can get; go as a bearer of wood, a drawer of water; do anything that you find that you can do. If you can find nothing else to do, take a loaf of bread and visit the poor widow, and the Lord will reward you. "He that watereth shall be watered also himself," and "the liberal soul shall be made fat."

My friends, if you want to get out of the misery and sorrow and gloom and sadness that are gathering around you, do something for the Lord. A woman came to me some time ago, with a scowl on her face. She said to me, "Mr. Moody, do you ever have any doubts?" I replied, "My good woman, I do not have any time for doubts. [Laughter.] If you work for the Lord you will have no time to doubt." It is the people who do nothing but talk to themselves and about themselves that have time to doubt. My dear friends, oh, look over the fields, and you will see them white for the harvest.

There was a nobleman in England in the last century. He got so that he looked upon life as such a heavy burden that finally he wanted to throw it away. He did not want to live any longer. But it happened that he was approached by a child begging for alms. He did not look at the child. He told him that there were eight of them in the family; that his father and mother was sick, and they were starving. He said to himself: "I might just as well give my pocket-book to the family, as I shall not want it any longer now;" and so he went to the house and said to them, "There, you can have all that is in it," and the tears sprang up into the eyes of the father and mother. They could hardly believe it. And the joy that was there so touched him that he said he would call again the next day; and he went there on the next day, and he became the most noted philanthropic man of his age, doing immense good. He was saved by his own good deed; and you may be saved; and there are many men and women in gloom and sorrow and misery and sadness who may do the work of the Lord, and He will lift them up to the peace and joy of heaven. My friends, there is plenty of room in this city. The fields are white for the harvest. I would say now that I have never seen a prouder day than this. I think I never saw a better night for the work of the Lord than last Sunday night at the North Side church. They knelt down before the Lord by hundreds. I believe there will be streams of salvation breaking out all over the city if the people will go forward in the work.

Shall we not take the city for Christ? Friends, let us preach and hold Him up. The world cannot go on without Christ. The world is perishing for the want of Christ. Let us preach Him at all seasons, in season and out of season, and the Lord will bless us if we go on.

Now, then, a great many people are afraid of being called peculiar. Now I would not give much for a man that is not peculiar in some way, I believe that old Enoch was the most peculiar man that ever lived. What kind of a man was he, was asked. Oh, a very good man, but he would not go to the theatre on Sunday or any other day. He wouldn't go to a horse race. He calls it an ungodly world. And so they called him a peculiar man; peculiar in the sight of the world. A good many say that they do not want to be called peculiar. If you had gone to some one in those old days and asked what they thought of Elijah, they would have said that Elijah was a good man enough, but he was a peculiar one. He would not bow himself to Baal. My friends, I would to God that we had many such men as Elijah with us now.

If you had gone down to Babylon in the days of Nebuchadnezzar and asked what kind of a man Daniel was, they would have answered you, "Oh, he is a good man enough. He is not a corrupt man. You could not bribe him, but he is a very peculiar man. He prays three times a day."

Now our business men in Chicago do not have time to pray three times a day. They have to go on 'Change and buy and bargain and make money and pile up millions. They say they have too much business to attend to to pray three times a day. But this man Daniel, who was the prime minister of that country and had all the business of the State to do, had time to pray three times a day; and who was the great man? He or they? Where are now the names of the merchant princes of Babylon, or their wise men? You don't know the name of one of them. All have faded away centuries ago; but the name of Daniel shines still brighter than ever; and they that turned away to rejoice in the Lord are, as the stars, forever and forever.

Dear friends, let us, as we hasten to go from this hall, say, "Lord, here am I, Lord, choose me. I lay myself at Thy feet—soul and body—a living sacrifice on the altar of God. Let me hear Thy voice sending me out into the white fields to work for Thy glory."

THIRD DAY OF THE CONVENTION.

MORNING SERVICE.

The day did not break auspiciously, but the third day and final sessions of the famous Christian Convention did—there was no storm inside. The usual vast crowd assembled, and the usual preliminary services of song as fitly led up to the work of the initial hour. Prayer was offered by the Rev. Mr. Stimpson, of Worcester, Mass., and inspiration for the day sought in that hymn of hope, "Sing Them Over Again to Me, Wonderful Words of Life." Prayer and still other singing ensued, Mr. Sankey conducting in "More Love to Thee." Mr. Moody then continued the services by announcing that Professor F. B. Fisk would read from the Scriptures. Professor Fisk chose the twelfth chapter of Romans, and forthwith read, at times making brief comments, those concise injunctions for the living of a godly life.

After the singing of "Nearer, my God, to Thee," and after Mr. Sankey had sung, by request, that beautiful number, "The Mists Have Rolled Away," effectively assisted by the congregation, Mr. Moody announced a necessary change in the programme, and in view of it introduced the Rev. Dr. Herrick Johnson, whose duties at the Theological Seminary demanded his being heard in the morning instead of the afternoon.

The topic was:

"HOW CAN THE PERSONAL AND SOCIAL STUDY OF THE BIBLE BE INCREASED?"

Rev. Dr. Johnson said: "How can the personal and social study of the Bible be increased?" is the way the question is put. I should prefer to put it, "How can the individual and associated study of the Bible be increased?" Let me be swift to say that it has increased in the last decade beyond all precedent, and is increasing. The surest road to future success is by the way of the recognition of the fact and method of past success. I am instant to say this because it has come to pass in our time that whenever any one stands up before an audience to speak in reference to the shadows that fall upon our world, and to picture somewhat the dark side of the truth, there is always some one ready to rush to the front and exclaim, "Behold, another pessimist come to judgment. Lo! we have a weeping bulrush, and now look out for the lamentation of Jeremiah."

That fellow evidently thinks that there is no study of the word of God, and he is blind to the facts of the hour: so I am swift to say that there is more study of the word of God than ever; that more millions bend over the word of God to-day, with eagerness to get at its contents, than have done so in any other age or hour of the world's history.

You may go anywhere and hear something about the facts of the Scripture. The best thoughts of the best men of the best races are gathering their utmost, and are thus increasing the volume bearing them into the track of Christ. Never before have there been so many facilities for the study of the word of God furnished, and such rare facilities offered as we have this very hour; and never so many have there been willing to employ these facilities for getting at the secrets and treasures of the holy word.

But saying this and understanding and believing this, it is nevertheless to be admitted that there are thousands upon thousands who never read the word, or read it only once a day; perhaps late at night when worn with the labors and toils of the day, yet not willing to sleep, and hardly daring to sleep, unless they have let their eyes go down a half page of Scriptures. There are thousands upon thousands in our Christian homes who read it only once a week—on the Sabbath perhaps, and in their secret hearts, believing that the Bible is, after all, a somewhat stupid book. There are thousands of thousands who used to read it every Sabbath, who now never read it, it being blanketed over with that great Sunday refuge from ennui, the Sunday morning newspaper, and the cause of so much weak, sickly, sentimental, formless, wishy-washy twaddle. The cause of so much instability in the Christian faith is a want of familiarity with this word of God. Nothing so largely puts good fiber into Christian manhood and womanhood as Scripture pabulum, and we cannot have the best of this sort of thing until we get a more thorough study of the word of God than we have to-day. And the cause of a great deal of the latent power in the church to-day—a power that I believe is yet to be developed over and above anything that has been developed in the past—is the want of familiarity with the Scriptures.

How, then, can the individual and associated study of the Bible be increased?

Let me say negatively, 1. By not minimizing its truth. We cannot crowd the word of God into "Come to Jesus" and say we are preaching the word of God. The commandments are as much a part of the word of God as any other portion. We cannot expect that all will honor God's word and secure its extended study and reading unless we are prepared to give it full and adequate proclamation; and it was my joy, therefore, in the opening session of this convention to hear Brother Whittle emphasize so distinctly the importance of convincing men that they are lost before they are ready to be saved. The Scriptures are a saving balm. But what is a balm for, except for a wounded member, and who will care anything about it unless he has one? The Scripture is a lullaby, but it is more than that. The word of God is quickening, living fire, sharper than any two-edged sword. Does the lullaby pierce? Is the sweet song a sword to the spirit? No. We must not minimize the truth if we are going to secure for the word of God more attentive reading and study.

In the second place, we are not going to secure its study by mutilating the Bible, tearing out sections and throwing away books. It is a poor way of getting a hearing for a book to tear it up into parts and shy leaves at a fellow [Laughter.] We cannot do what we want by tossing away Moses, and flaunting at Paul, and eulogizing Jesus alone. If the Old Testament must go the New Testament must go, too. Moses and Jesus and Paul must stand or fall together. Deuteronomy and Ezra and the Gospels and Epistles must stand or fall together. For beginning at Moses and the prophets the same story extends all through the Bible. The crimson thread of the Old Testament and the crimson thread of the New Testament, each dyed in the blood of Calvary, are seen, and that thread stretches from Moses to John, from John to Revelation, and all along upon that thread are strung the connecting links of history. The course of prophecy and history are one and what God has joined let no man tear apart. Not by mutilating the Bible are we going to secure the more general reading of the Bible.

Next, not by theories of its origin which put it on the level of the purest naturalism can the individual and associated study of the Bible be increased. Those books which constitute the Bible are not a natural development in the order of nature. They did not grow like Topsy. They were made—made in sections by the hand of God, through His spirit working on in the minds of men. The inspiration of Moses is not the inspiration of Newton. Paul did not speak as Confucius, or Zoroaster, or Vishnu, or Socrates spoke. The men of the New Testament spoke like those of the Old Testament, for they spoke by the Holy Ghost. The men of the New Testament said that they come with the wisdom that the Holy Ghost teaches; the men of the Old Testament spake from God himself. And so we must elevate the Bible up to this high level and keep it there if we would give it more general reading.

Now, to take the positive side:

By writing better living epistles we are to secure an increased study of the word of God, individually and associated, by writing better living epistles. We, in our lives as Christians, ought to be a perfect transcript of the word of God. Are we? We know how very far short we fall from being that, and yet there is no better way by which we can emphasize and command attention for the word of God than to put that word into a life.

We have heard a great deal recently about a new translation of the New Testament, and I am one of those who rejoice in the "revision." We need it, and ought to have it. I welcome and indorse and believe in it. But the translation I believe to be most needed is the translation of the word of God into action—living "epistles," that shall tell to men everywhere what the truth is.

The walking epistle goes everywhere. You can go into the business place, the mart, everywhere, and walk the gospel right into the eye and the heart of man, for you walk into them.

Mr. Moody said, and I echoed the remark because I thought it wonderfully in the line of my own thought, and adapted to the occasion, though used in a different connection—he said one of the most humiliating things in the church is that there are so many portions of it who have no testimony. What is that but saying that if we are going to send out this gospel and get men interested in it we must put it into ourselves, and not do with it as if it were something for our own experience alone. We should make men look upon it. Look at that motto, "Your body is the temple of the Holy Ghost." Oh! if this mass of Christians are to-day to realize that—not simply to their own timid consciences, not so that a feeble hope could be born from it, but so that men should be made to believe it. Oh! that the Christian could see as each one walked the street, the temple of the Holy Ghost. Oh! how the streets would be crowded to find out where the cause of this power was.

Again, we may increase the study, individual and associated, of the word of God by better methods in the household. Here is a little child—you have often seen such a beautiful sight—nestled in his mother's arms, hearing a Bible story, the story of Moses, the story of Joseph, the story of Abraham, the story of Paul in prison, the story of the shipwreck, those inimitable stories of Jesus told in parable, and those other inimitable stories—parables in action—called His miracles. The Scripture is full of them, of just such stories; and that child, with open eye, and mouth, and ear, takes in the beautiful stories, listening with eager, wondering interest, and asking the mother to tell some old, old story, over again. The child never tires of it. See that boy. He is 16 or 18 years of age. What interest has he in the word of God? He has grown from babyhood into manhood. He is in the same Christian home; and yet if you will shut in such a young man who listened so eagerly to the stories of the Scripture when he was a child—if you will shut this young man up with an almanac, a directory and a Bible, he will turn over the pages of the first for a few minutes; do the same with the second, but he will almost die before he will look at the Bible.

What is the trouble. It is because he has become—been made—disgusted with the Scriptures. And yet Milton and Newton and a host of other great men have kept the Bible ever before them, and satisfied the calls of their intellect by going to the word of God for inspiration and pabulum. Well, we must attribute something of the trouble to the actual prejudices of the human heart. They have been developed from time to time, and if he has not been converted, they continue to increase. But I tell you the boy has not been treated rightly in connection with the Bible. He has been taught to consider its reading as a system of tasks, and he has been compelled, with his father and mother to go through the tiresome genealogies chapter by chapter, one chapter a day, from Moses to Revelation. Oh! it seems to me if we want to keep our young men in the household familiar with the Scriptures, in love with them, and glad to read them, we must not have any rigid order for their reading it. Free it from the idea of a task. And I feel sure if this were done we should have more Bible-reading in our homes.

Here is a field filled with the odors of sweet blossoms, and you must cultivate it. Then, I say, that we should give more notice to our methods in the household.

My third point is that, in order to increase the study of the Scriptures in an individual and associated way, we should have better methods in the pulpit, and here, of course, I am speaking to myself as well as to others in the ministry. I believe that there is a great deal of preaching not at all adapted to secure readers for the Scriptures and make men in love with it. It is in this way that the text is sometimes read at the beginning and that is the last heard of it.

Another method is to take a text and stick to it, but he only thumps and bumps at it. It is a repetition of the text turned up and down in various forms. That is the sermon, but there is not any gospel in it. He has simply given the text and verbal emphasis as he has thumped down the words. Suppose we treated any other book in that way, and professed to be one who was going to teach a great deal of Shakespeare, for instance, and we took my "kingdom for a horse" for a text, and that is the last we say about the king and the horse he wants. That would be one way

Or suppose we take the other way to teach Shakespeare, with the same text. You commence, "Well, we will discuss the nature of a king, and say something about a king. My second point is a horse, the fine points of a horse, the relation of a king to a horse." How much of Shakespeare is going to be taught in that way. Is not that the way in which the word of the Lord is often preached, and is that method the best way of increasing the interest in the word? What is the best method of increasing the interest in the word of God? It is to tell people to go and seek for themselves after new riches in the word of the Lord.

It was my pleasure to follow Albert Barnes as his successor—all honor to his blessed memory. It was his habit, Sabbath after Sabbath, year after year, to explain the Scriptures, to take passages at considerable length and unfold their meaning ; to show their drift and their tendency and their fullest meaning ; and the result was that I found in the church men and women who knew far more of the word of God than I did ; who were familiar with the sacred history from beginning to end, who were in the habit of talking about it day by day, for they had been taught by that good man of God to do so by his preaching and by the manner of his preaching. Before God, I believe, if we want to have more study of God's word, we must show by this connected way of preaching what the way is.

Look at Scotland, remarkable for its knowledge of the word of God—a knowledge attained largely through this method of teaching ; by multiplying the means for unlocking the secrets of the Bible, and disclosing its treasures of thought and sentiment and poetry, its sublimities, its glories, its pathos, its blessed facts and revelations ; keeping ever high above all other thoughts, the fact that the Bible is a divine revelation of God's word. Above all I would say keep before you the purpose to make men believe that this word of God is not only the best history ; not only the best poetry the world can show in all literature, but beyond all and over all, that it is a divine revelation, thrilling through all its nervous words with the inspiration of Jehovah. [Applause].

A hymn, " My Jesus, I love Thee," was sung at the conclusion of Dr. Johnson's address, and Mr. Moody at once introduced Mr. B. F. Jacobs, who was appointed for a ten-minute talk on this same subject of Bible study.

Mr Jacobs began by saying, it had been said that the written word of God was treated now as was the living word when Christ was upon the earth. The problem to be considered was how to overcome the neglect of, rather than the opposition to, the word of God. To attain this end the speaker first recommended some change in the treatment of the Bible in public worship, at which time he deprecated the putting of the hymn-book so far in advance of the Bible. He did not altogether approve of the method of the Episcopalians, who incorporate a fragment of Scripture with the prayer book or with the hymns.

He believed that better and the best results would ensue from a more liberal use of the Bible in the worship of God.

Again, he believed that the word of God should have place in the prayer meeting. He declared, and his declaration evoked most audible approval, that the Bible ought to be used in the Sunday school and not lesson papers or question books. He reproved those rich churches which neglect to furnish the Bible to their mission schools. He affirmed that the Bible should be used in family worship and not Spurgeon's "Gems," or "Ray's Morning Exercises." Many a young man was setting up his family altar who vitally needed to be shown the use of the sacred word.

Mr. Jacobs, in passing, showed what noble examples for those sustaining the various relations of family life were contained in the Bible lessons that are being taught in the Sunday school. He spoke of the praying mother of Samuel, conscious of the truth that character is transmittable, who prayed before her son was born and after his coming had blessed her prayers. He incidentally touched upon the little lessons of life, that the boy Samuel, in his various services, preached for the children of all time.

He emphasized the need of organizing Bible bands, by which agency, while the family is assigned its daily chapter, the little child, too, is not omitted, but is given its tiny verse.

As another aid to social Bible study, he asked why there might not be established in different parts of the city reading clubs for Bible study, as there were clubs for the profitable and pleasurable reading of other literature. For what treasures there were to be mined! Poetry, biography, history were there in beautiful abundance. Again, might not the ladies of the congregations go into the houses of this city, carrying the word of God, as was done after Miss Dryer's plan? To further promote the study of the Bible personal diligence was necessary, for the Bible was a personal book all the way through. God reached His people through His people, one by one. The Bible was the palace beautiful. If it was opened at random and aid sought and none came, perhaps many a poor soul wondered why the Lord did not meet his need. But the help was there; just the right kind for every one.

Prayer by Dr. Hatfield followed the remarks of Mr. Jacobs.

The topic for 11 o'clock was,

"HOW MAY OUR FOREIGN POPULATION BE EVANGELIZED?"

The Rev. F. E. Emerich said he had lived for many years in a German home, and he had for that reason been selected to speak on this question. God had wonderfully blessed America in bringing to its shores the peoples from every country on the globe. God had given America a heritage and a privilege of working for Him that had been accorded to no other people.

It had been said that in this country there was to be enacted the modern Pentecost—when all the peoples of the world would be brought together to hear the word of God.

There was no difficulty in reaching the Scotch, English and Welsh people by American methods, because they were so near akin to ourselves that our methods reached them. But what were we to do for the Germans and Scandinavians. In his church, Mr. Emerich said he had thirteen different nationalities on the church rolls but the greater portion of them were Scandinavians. He found no difficulty in reaching these people because they had been taught by our methods. They had been reared in the grand old Lutheran Church, and they had a great love for the memory of Luther. They had been brought up in a Christian faith. In asking the question of what should be done for the Germans, we should remember not so much the infidelity and rationalism of the Germany of to-day, but more the Germany of Luther, whose 400th anniversary was to be celebrated this year. Could these people be evangelized? Luther had worked out his reformation by faith. We should remember this, and that the great Wesley had drawn his power to evangelize from German sources. If the German had not the gospel in its churches it had the power of the gospel in its church hymns, which had been translated into almost every tongue, and were in fact our greatest power for evangelization.

The evangelist need not give up hope for these people.

The Methodists were doing a grand work among these people, and giving the Germans a literature that would bring good fruit. Then there was the Lutheran Church, which had reached the Germans in its own way, and if we would remember the religious history of Germany rather than its infidelity, and take hope to work with them, they could be evangelized.

But how were they to be reached?

First, we must acknowledge the work that was being done among the Germans to-day. They had a love for the old mother church of Luther. It was making itself manifest this year more than for many years. The Germans loved that church. We must acknowledge the work that church was doing in this country and at home. It ranked third in the great evangelical churches, only the Methodist and Baptist standing ahead of it. The church workers of this country could not afford to fail to give recognition to such a power for Christ. What if it did not have the same methods we employed? The old notions that had clung to the Lutheran church would drop off when it had become somewhat Americanized. We should remember that the Baptists had stood where the Lutherans did a century ago, but they had seen their mistakes when Edwards and Whitfield gave them the proof. Why should not we be as hopeful concerning the Lutherans?

As much could be done with the German churches as had been done with others.

When the revival of God's spirit came upon them they would speak the truth. They would learn as the American church had learned to preach the gospel free from dogma. We needed patience with these German Christians.

The speaker had been greatly impressed with the patience of God with Israel. We needed the spirit of Christ, and we needed to remember what the Apostle Paul said about the patience of Christ. The Germans came to this country with prejudices, and these must be overcome. They came with un-American ideas concerning the observance of the Sabbath and temperance. We should remember that our ideas of these questions were as strange to them as were their ideas to us. They had followed Calvin and Luther, and believed they were right in their way. Mr. Emerich said, as for himself, he had lived twenty years in a German home and learned the customs of the people, but he had afterward lived for sixteen years in the homes of New England, and he had now but one idea of Sabbath observance, and that was the New England way.

He knew the German way and the New England way, and he could look at the question from the German standpoint. He knew how long it took him to learn that he must not buy on the Sabbath day. He had no idea that he was breaking the fourth commandment until his old teacher kindly pointed it out to him. Many of these German people had never once had presented to them from the standpoint of love, the fourth commandment. They should put in the leaven of God's truth and it would do the work.

Then in answering the question of how to reach the foreign population, he would say, by recognizing what work had already been done for the Germans, and by working in harmony with the foreign pastors, helping them with sympathy and practical efforts. We needed to have faith in the power of Christian community and fellowship. Another way was to reach the foreign population through the children. These people wanted their children confirmed, and they were much more careful about teaching them the Scriptures than were our own people.

"HOW TO REACH THE GERMANS."

The Rev. Lee M. Heilman, of Grace English Lutheran Church, spoke as follows:

To evangelize all our foreign population would, in a large measure, revolutionize our courts of justice, our social life, and general political and religious institutions. To bring under the power of the gospel all the various nations and tongues of our land and make them speak for Christ would be to convert Babel into a Pentecost, and nations among us would be born in a day. There is, perhaps, no topic that can claim the serious attention of such an assembly more profitably than this, for on the solution of it hangs on the one hand the future of our land and the permanence of its free institutions, and on the other hand assurance that here shall not be left another district of Christ's church turned into heathen, Asia Minor with no cross left. While these hundreds of thousands are coming annually to us, we need inquire how the godlessness, the rationalism, formalism and infidelity poured upon us shall be made to disenthrall great talent and turn it to the Master's service.

It is, however, only just that I should protest against the too prevalent idea among us Americans, that there is almost no piety among those of any other than the English speech. I speak for Scandinavians and some Protestant Germans. Still that does not change the fact that of these very nations, and many others more or less foreign, are many hundreds neglecting their dearest interests and thousands more of them doing violence to the kingdom of God.

To reach these with the saving grace of Calvary is of course to reach souls in a common fallen race. There is but one Jesus, one gospel, and one spirit of regeneration, to touch on the mainspring of human want. The solution of the problem in hand lies in how this Christ, the wisdom and the power of God, shall be brought to this foreign population. This class of people has not been generally reached, and there are reasons for it, and these furnish the answers *how* to bring them more to a knowledge of the truth.

There is, for example, in Chicago but one church for about every 4,000 Protestant Germans and Scandinavians. There are Lutheran pastors, it is estimated, who have in their parishes at least 1,500 families. No church or pastor can there minister to the sick and dying, and meet all other demands, and then yet properly cultivate the field. Hence it is, many have only a nominal relation to the church by their occasional attendance of their children at the schools and the burying of their dead by the pastor. Is it any wonder that the best are tempted to careless and bad habits, and that many are led to vice and clothe a quaking conscience with scepticism? Church life and influence, and the word of God are wanting, and there the heart left without the ordained safeguards is as uncertain of its course as is the serpent coiled on the rock. Home life is soon demoralized and the young left unrestrained are reared, especially in their idling Sabbath hours and at nights, for every vice of tongue, eye and palate. With not room enough in churches, and not sufficient agencies to win the non-church-going young men of Catholic, Protestant and no persuasion, and of all languages, the field brings forth our most dangerous and Godless classes.

Again, however, I remark, the foreign population must not be treated as a charity people. To build them churches, and have some Americans at stated times take the part of workers among them will never get into the heart of their real thousands. Money and prayers have done great things, but proxy methods are not enough. God's plan is to have churches where all classes actually unite into one association. Besides, He appoints pastors who must have the "care of souls and the oversight of the flock." They are to be among them like the physician, for every emergency. The pastoral element is divinely chosen, and there is no eloquence, or learning, or any form of proper evangelization that can safely take the place of its office to care for the sick, the dying, visiting the doubting and backsliding, or preaching from house to house the cross of Jesus. Let all other agencies do their part but you cannot sustain a church work properly except by a "house-going pastor," who makes a permanent and "church going people" Do not, especially, seek to reach the foreign population by proxy only, for if there is not a nearer touch of heart to heart, they will feel the work as a kind of charity, and that feeling tends to depress rather than to lift up and inspire.

Then, again, there must be a care for their Americanizing. The question of language, nationality, and habits presents enormous difficulties. Let the old people have the gospel in their mother tongue, but have not for their leaders and ministers the unprogressive who are sticklers for the forms, and seek to propagate the formalism and spirit of their native countries. Give them men of this modern age and who are filled with the spirit of regeneration and of moral reform in Sabbath keeping, temperance, and the general good of men. My observation has taught me that there are ministers and people in various denominations, no matter what earnest professsions they make, who, rather than leave their own habits and tongue and their church, or suffer their English speaking children to do so, will let the church die and their youths sent into the world. There is special need to care for the more liberal and anglicized. There are towns and large districts in the city where are no English churches.

Suffer me, however, to present this antithesis as a next remark: These people ought not be too readily deprived of their own churches unless they adhere to an unevangelical branch or prefer another. Great harm and confusion have been thus often caused and more souls sent from the cross than brought to it. If they are Methodists across the sea let them be that there. If they are German Reformed, or Lutheran, or Presbyterian, or Congregational, they are reached and preserved far more easily in their own home, if possible. Believe me as speaking from honest conviction and knowledge on this point, and out of mercy for the souls concerned. It is a duty to be wise as well as faithful, like Paul, who, to win the formalistic Pharisee, claimed himself to be of them. I know, some will be doubtful about the Lutheran and Reformed, and perhaps the German Evangelical Union, but there are evangelical branches of them, notably of the first named who are Americanized, pietistic, and claim such men as Spener, Tholuck, Luthhardt, and Christlieb, and their success, where they have been permitted to go, is proof of this point. Go, however, my brother, and in any church and way save the fallen and unreached thousands of all classes.

Once more, I remark, the young people should be brought into the church, whatever that church. It is not enough to gather them into the Sunday school, but when really brought to a personal Savior let them profess Him and take on them the decided and whole armor of the Christian life. In 1865 the Rev. Mr. Punshon said in England that when Newcastle-on-Tyne, which was a very hot bed of infidelity, was canvassed, "it was found that nine-tenths of the most prominent members of the infidel clubs had passed through their Sabbath schools." If you would really reach them, and through them the older, bring them into full church life.

In a word, let us be consecrated in any way to save these hearts athirst for the water of life. Let our work be popular and plainly preach repentance and a living faith. Let us tenderly mingle among them and learn to appreciate them, and so compel the worst to find Christ the real want of the soul. Aid our Sabbath Association and Young Men's Christian Association. Let us by our holy lives convince the skeptic of the power of our religion, and by our real brotherly union of all churches disarm the assault that we are really at war among ourselves. We should remember that all tongues are of one parentage and alike sinful, and that one Jesus alone can heal the wound of death.

Professor Samuel Ives Curtiss, of the Chicago Theological Seminary, in discussing this subject further, said he would first present a few figures. Illinois had a native population of 2,494,294 and a foreign population of 583,576; Minnesota had a native population of 513,097 and a foreign population of 267,276; Wisconsin had a native population of 910,072 and a foreign population of 405,425; Chicago had a total population of 503,185, according to the census of 1880, and of this 204,859 were foreign born.

He then spoke as follows:

I will first speak of some of the hindrances to the evangelization of those Germans who were born in Germany, because of their education and surroundings in that country.

1. The State has said, until recently, to all parents in Germany, You must have your children baptized. The fathers might say, But I don't believe in Christianity; I don't believe there is a God. The State has said it makes no difference. It is the law that every Protestant and Catholic child should be baptized; bring your child or we will fine you.

2. The State has said, until recently, every boy and girl of the age of thirteen or fourteen must be confirmed. Here again the parents might say, "But we do not believe in Christianity." The State has said, "I cannot help that. Your boy or girl cannot enter upon an occupation without a certificate that they are members of the State church.

3. The State says you may not leave the church, and elect any pastor you choose. With me rests the nomination of your pastor. He is, to a certain extent, a State official.

What is the result of this? An estrangement of the masses in the cities and towns from the ministry. Many a German says, the minister does not care anything about me. He only cares for my money. When my boy is baptized it means a fee; when he is confirmed, another fee; when sickness invades my family, more fees, and when death comes, other fees. Some pay them loyally. A pastor in Leipzig once told me the story of a peasant who wished to help his father, who was poor, and had a large family. He came to him and said: "Pastor, I want you should write my funeral sermon, and I will pay for it." In due time it was written and paid for. After a time the peasant, seeing his pastor was not getting on very well, came and said: "Pastor, I want you should write a funeral sermon for my wife, and I will pay you for it." It was prepared, and so he went through the whole family.

The minister is not to blame. He says: "Here I am, with my three colleagues, with a parish of 40,000 on my hands. What can we do? I would gladly do more. My heart yearns for the people. The church building was erected by the State, and it was built to last. The dust of ages is in it. It is like being in a charnel house to attend service in it—cold, dark, gloomy. Are the people there? No, they are in the sunny fields, listening to music in the gardens, and at evening attending the schools of wit in the theater."

Now, can you wonder that the natural tendency for the majority of Germans when they come to this country is to throw aside these irksome restraints? How many thousands upon thousands of native-born Americans who have been connected with pleasant churches at the East, cease to be church members when they go

West, and thus fall into indifferentism? But this is far more true of the Germans who come to this country.

1. The lack of vital piety among many of the ministers.

Religion is too often a matter of the head rather than of the heart. It is taught in the schools like arithmetic and grammar, and too often by men who are unbelievers.

Piety, a change of heart, is not at all necessary for a student of theology. The ministry is a profession like law and medicine, and it is too often the case that the men who cannot pass the terribly strict examination for the legal profession, or think they cannot, study for the ministry.

The students are more characterized for ochsen and kneipen, as they call it, than for religious work. Not more than 60 out of the 600 theological students in Leipzig are engaged in practical Christian work. I will not deny that the German church furnishes some of the most devoted Christian pastors, but the system of religious education, although in many respects valuable, is stunted and neutralized to a great extent by this unbelieving atmosphere. The effect of this upon all Germans who have been under this influence is to cause them to be satisfied with a dead name.

It was a standard question at the tax office when I resided in Leipzig, whether the tax payers were Evangelical, Catholic or Jewish. Everybody is either Jew or Christian, and if brother Moody were to preach among the Germans, and hold an after-meeting, and were to put the question to man or woman, are you a Christian, the invariable answer would be, certainly. He would mean, have you been born again? They would mean that they had been baptized, were members of the national church and had been educated in the truths of religion.

This constitutes a tremendous obstacle in reaching the people who have been under such training when they have come to this country.

2. Another hindrance is in Sabbath desecration.

The German habit of making the Sabbath a holiday instead of a holy day is one of the greatest obstacles to the evangelization of Germans, whether in the fatherland or in this country.

The church can never be a power in this or that land when the Sabbath is given up to worldly pursuits and pleasures. God must have all or none. The ride for health, the friendly call, the journey that ends Sunday morning or begins Sunday evening are the camel's head, which will finally be followed by his whole body. The Sabbath must be kept as the grand field day for the church, or religion will be weak and sickly.

Now Leipzig, where I resided five years, is estimated to have a population of 200,000. It has seven churches. It has perhaps three stirring preachers, but they do not preach every Sunday. They alternate with colleagues, who have but little power to arouse the people. I am sure, from my own observation, that an average attendance of 3,500 to 4,000 a Sunday would be very large in Leipzig; that would leave 196,000 non-church goers. But this summer, when I was there, on one of the Sundays 40,000 people left on excursion trains for various resorts in the neighborhood. Can religion be a power under such circumstances? Can such a Sabbath be a field day for the church? When in the whirl of the business and pleasures of this life is room to be found to follow in the sorrowful footsteps of our Lord who came to die for this world?

This is a tremendous hindrance to the evangelization of the Germans.

Now, how shall we evangelize them? I must confess that my heart yearns for them. I lived among them six years. Three of my children were born among them. All that is mortal of one sleeps in a German burying-ground. But I feel that I have no wisdom in this matter. I have had no practical experience in the work among them.

I will, however, venture to offer the following suggestions as to those who work among them:

1. The ministers and evangelists who labor among them must be consecrated, devoted men. No man is fit for the work who thinks he can get a living in that way better than in any other, or who proposes to make his work a stepping stone to anything else. Men's hearts should be on fire with love for the work. They should be ready to say within themselves, woe is me if I preach not the gospel to them.

Men cannot resist the power of divine love as communicated through human speech, and exemplified in a human life.

Ministers and evangelists may get a hearing when speaking in a foreign tongue through an interpreter, or when using the language imperfectly. Mutual love and confidence will cover up a multitude of defects. But there is a more excellent way than to speak to them in a foreign language.

2. They should themselves be foreign-born and be able to speak German with fluency and correctness.

The prophet says in Is. xi., 1, according to the Hebrew, "Speak ye to the heart of Jerusalem." If you wish to touch the hearts of people, speak to them in the tongue in which they were born, waken some sleeping memory of a praying mother, of a faithful pastor. Let your language be that of sacred recollection, and that which men use when they are dying, and you will have the last medium of touching their hearts.

3. They should know the history and customs of the people.

It is not enough that a man should be a German to speak to Germans. He must know the glories of the fatherland. He must know her patriots and statesmen. While he ought to be an American through and through, he ought to be able to kindle into patriotic devotion when he hears such German songs as "The Watch on the Rhine."

He ought to know not only that Germany had a Martin Luther, but what Martin Luther did, and what Germany has been and is to-day for the religious thinking of the world. He ought to know their social customs, and remember that the practice of using wine and beer among the pastors and Christian people in Germany is much the same as it was among our Puritan ancestors seventy-five years ago. We should be patient and very charitable as to these things.

4. They should avoid as far as possible antagonism to the historical churches. In their own bosom (that is of the churches) the powers are yet to work most effectually for the evangelization of Germany. To treat them, therefore, as foes is to wound Christ in the house of His friends. Let us fellowship with them so far as they will allow it, going two-thirds or the whole of the way if necessary to clasp hands.

5. Other churches which are not national may engage in this work. Like the Dissenters in England, they may stir up the old historic church to new life and energy.

In any case, this work should go forth from the church, and should return thither. For Christ loved the church and gave Himself for it, and we are one with Him when we try to promote the efficiency and spirituality of that body of which He Himself is the head.

THE NOON MEETING.

The noon prayer meeting was simply a continuation of the morning session, as many people coming in as there were those that retired. Mr. Moody requested the audience to sing hymn No. 71, "How Sweet the Name of Jesus Sounds."

Dr. Moorhouse then offered prayer, and was followed by Brother Millard in another prayer, after which the hymn No. 87, "Lord, I Hear of Showers of Blessings," was sung.

The Rev. Dr. Arthur Little read Psalm 24, "Who shall ascend into the hill of the Lord? or, who shall stand in His holy place?"

"He that hath clean hands, and a pure heart; who hath not lifted up his soul unto vanity; nor sworn deceitfully." "Search me, Oh, God, and know my heart."

In other words, my beloved friends, it has been my privilege to be a listener here, and not a speaker, said Dr. Little. I have come to see that, if this convention has done any good to me, I must humble myself, and as I go to God's temple from day to day and week to week, see that I have clean hands and a clean heart. In the last three days this convention has proved that there was a terrible deficiency on the part of the Christian churches and workers. If there is not an honest effort made on the part of professing Christians to bring in the thousands in the suburbs of the large cities who never enter the Lord's house, it is useless to have brought Brother Moody here at all.

Brother Moody then offered a prayer, in which he invoked the Lord's aid in assisting the people and clergymen of this city to come to the temple with clean hearts and hands. He asked God to grant that the reports of this convention, as published in the press of Chicago, be efficient in stirring up a Christian feeling in the hearts of those in distant portions of the land, so that a wave of Christian salvation might sweep over the country, as it did in 1857 and 1858.

Hymn No. 77, "Sweet Hour of Prayer," was sung by the audience with a right good will.

Brother Moody then related a story of a family in England who had an erring son in Australia who was saved through the prayers of his mother in England.

Fred Riebold, from Dayton, Ohio, related the manner of his conversion some fourteen months ago, and how the love of God completely filled his being now.

Major Whittle spoke in reference to Riebold, who, he said, was one of the speculating and fast class of men in Dayton, and one of a syndicate that manipulated a railroad. All this he had given up for God's work. Major Whittle then offered a prayer, and the closing anthem, "Praise God, from whom all blessings flow" was sung.

The benediction was offered by Dr. Bascom, and the immense throng filed out of the hall.

AFTERNOON SESSION.

There were several hundred people who never left the hall between the morning and the afternoon sessions, but sacrificed their lunches rather than lose their seats for the afternoon, and those who did leave had their places taken by others as fast as they were made vacant. At 2 o'clock Mrs. McGranahan, presiding at the organ, led the vast audience in singing several gospel hymns. Mr. Moody came in a few minutes before the time for opening the convention, and was kept busy looking over notes sent to him. He requested Mr. and Mrs. McGranahan to sing "The Two Lives." It was a touching song, telling the simple story of two lives representing the two extremes of society—the rich and the poor. So widely separated in this world, they both lay in the Savior's arms at death, and "none could tell which had lived in the terrace house and which in the street below."

No one was more affected by this little song than the man who had requested that it be sung. Mr. Moody sat there with a look of sorrow on his face as the story of earthly trials was told in song, but as the distinction between the two lives was wiped out at death, there came a smile stealing over his face until there was a look of complete and perfect happiness there. The face was an indicator of the heart of the man, and the people noticed this and knew that Moody was a man of great heart and deep feeling.

After a prayer by Dr. Henson, Mr. McGranahan and his wife sung "We shall be satisfied."

Mr. Moody said there had been some complaint from those holding tickets that they had not been able to get into the meeting the night before. The committee were not to blame for this, because so many people without tickets gathered about the doors that the ticket-holders could not get near. The result was that some got in without tickets and some holding tickets were kept out. As the next session would be the last, the rush would probably be greater than ever, so it would be well for every one to look out for himself and not depend too much upon tickets.

Mr. Moody said: I am going to bring a charge against the ministers. They don't want children in the church during the service.

Dr. Hatfield—I deny the charge. I invite my people to bring the children to the services.

Dr. Humphrey—I know a man who not only invites the children to his church, but he gives them note-books and pencils and offers prizes of Bibles to those who will take down and remember the text.

Dr. Goodman—Yes; and I saw that man present thirty-nine Bibles to a class of boys, and I observed that he had 450 children out of the 600 in his Sabbath school in his church. And I resolved that I would try the same thing and see if I could not do as well. I am going to try it.

Dr. Henson—I get tired of preaching to the old saints and sinners and want young hearers. I encourage the children to come and hear me.

Another minister said: "I believe that the church should be put ahead of the Sunday school even in our talk to children."

Another said: "I invite my children not only to the church service but to the prayer meeting."

Still another: "I am always glad to see the children at all services. We want the infantry in God's army."

J. H. Walker said: "I deny the charge too. I urge my people to bring the children, and I say to them that they have no business in the house of God without their children. And last Sunday morning I had the accompaniment of a crying baby all through my sermon, but it did not disturb me."

Dr. Johnson—Mr. Moody, you will have to withdraw that charge.

Mr. Moody—Well, I will take that back, but I will make another. They don't give the children anything when they do come. [Laughter.]

Dr. Kendall—See here, Mr. Moody, I have always stood by you, but I won't do so any longer if you do not speak the truth.

Mr. Moody—Don't I speak it. Do you give them anything?

Dr. Kendall—I don't know. I believe I do. At least, I try to. I am reforming, or trying to. I have found I could give the parents some good hard hits when I was talking to the children.

And so the brisk cross-firing continued, one or two other platform speakers good-naturedly shooting their personal experiences at Mr. Moody. He faced the interesting fusilade that he had drawn out, with his back to the audience and his stanch and portly form seeming big enough to stand a broadside of the kind of bombardment he had provoked.

The firing slackening up Mr. Moody threw in a bit of his own experience. He said that he was seventeen years of age before he had heard a solitary word addressed to children. He recollected that for seventeen years he had thus heard nothing that was intended for him and his like, and that, at that age, he was waked up one day in church because he snored so loud. With such youthful memories he was glad that the ministers were devoting five minutes to children's talks. Some time ago, continued the ready evangelist, there was a man who was asked how it was that he had such fine sheep. He replied that it was because he looked after the lambs. So, said Mr. Moody, look after the children. All in the same vein of illustration and comment Mr. Moody told of a bit of a sermon that a little six-year-old girl, in imitation of the firstly, secondly, etc., method of her father had produced. Firstly, she said:

"The Lord loves us very, very much."

Secondly. "But He does not like us to sin."

Thirdly. "Don't you want to love Him."

Fourthly. "Lord have mercy on us."

Still talking for and about the children, an aged, white-haired pastor briefly referred to his successful work among the young people during his pastorate in Cincinnati, and said that when Christ came and made promises of salvation He put into these promises salvation for two—the believer and his offspring. So, concluded the venerable speaker, when I see a child backslide I feel as guilty for that child as when I first repented myself. After another clerical brother had given his particular experience on this children's topic, Mr. Sankey suggested that there be sung a children's hymn, which was done, number 97 being selected. Dr. Johnson followed in prayer, and there was sung, "Behold what love, what boundless love." "The Rock of Ages" was then sent swelling upward, for Mr. Moody wanted the singing of an old church hymn to open the discussion upon the question of church music.

"HOW SHALL WE INTEREST OUR CHILDREN IN THE GOSPEL?"

Rev. E. C. Ray, pastor of Presbyterian Church, of Hyde Park, spoke as follows:

The same old gospel that has been preached from Eden down. The same child-nature in Cain and Abel and our babies. The same old promise, "Train up a child in the way he should go, and when he is old he will not depart from it." A good missionary's bad son came to Christ late in life. His old mother said, "I expected it; I always believed the promise, 'Train up a child in the way he should go, and when he is *old* he will not depart from it.'" We take the promise otherwise. There is only one way—Christ. We believe that if we train up our children in Christ they will never depart from Him, never need to come back from sin to Him in old age. Now what characteristics of child-nature must we consider in order so to present the gospel that they shall be savingly, permanently interested in it?

In working iron we use tools various. But fire to soften comes first. Love is the force to make human nature plastic. We must love the child not only when fresh, rosy, bright, sweet, and clean; but when dirty, sick, ignorant, dull, cross. Love it because to despise one of these little ones is to despise Christ; love it for what it is in the kingdom of heaven, in the slums, in the present, in the future. Such love never faileth. It is a force which makes the child-heart soft for our molding. As God begins to interest us in the gospel by loving us, so we must begin with the little ones.

And then the gospel must be addressed to their affections. That gate into the child-heart stands always wide open. Take the truth in by that gate. Longfellow, in his poem to the children, said:

> "The heart hath its own memory, like the mind,
> And in it are enshrined
> The precious keepsakes, into which are wrought
> The giver's loving thought."

A little London girl who took the prize for a fine house plant, was asked how it thrived so in her narrow garret room. "I moved it around in the sun all day," she said. Keep the child-heart in the love of God. That love is a force; heat is a mode of motion. Show the gospel as it is, lovely. Make Sunday lovely. Make church services lovely. Make home religion lovely. Plant the incorruptible seed in the affections. You can't interest a child in philosophical religion or in sour religion. A child in a household where there is not the joy of the Holy Ghost is like a tender plant in a cellar.

And love alone can interest children in gospel work. Dr. C. S. Robinson says: "I once promised to help a disabled shoemaker with work. The friend who asked me, a New York merchant, walked six miles that winter night to cheer the poor fellow's heart with the news. If ever I straightened myself up to do something for another it was when I heard that. A man loved him; then so did I." The pitying love of God for the lost; the cross with its extended arms, embracing all races; your own earnest desire to save souls; these will interest the children in gospel work. Draw out a full clear note from your violin and the harp in the corner will echo it. There are tender strings in the child-heart that wait to be sympathetically awakened.

Wordsworth, reviewing his childhood, found this:

> "Heaven lies all about us in our infancy;
> Shades of the prison house begin to close
>   Upon the growing boy;
> But he beholds the light, and whence it flows,
>   He sees it in his joy;
> The youth who daily farther from the East
> Must travel, still is nature's priest.
>   And by the vision splendid
>   Is on his way attended;
> At length the man perceives it die away
> And fade into the common light of day.

Imagination belongs to childhood and youth. The child-hunger for Arabian Nights, Munchausen, Grimm, and Hans Christian Andersen is from above, heaven-sent. The strong, vivid imagination which makes a princess of a soiled rag doll, and of some old boards a palace, must be utilized in interesting the child in the gospel. Those Old Testament stories—we have to cudgel our brains sometimes to get homiletics out of them and to keep the critics' hands off—the children love them. That is how the Bible gets hold of them. Biography, which makes so large a part of the word, and modern biography, are inexhaustible stores of food for child piety. Stories of martyrs and of missionaries, and little stories of Christian children, and stories illustrating all the phases of gospel truth, are the natural food of the young. The common sneer against Sunday school story-books seems to me a curl of the lip of ignorance. Why do not such forbid Mr. Moody to use anecdotes? Because "without a parable spake He not unto them." Above all, the story of Jesus—it runs from Genesis to Revelation. A mother returning from communion told her curious children the story of the Last Supper. She illustrated on the sofa how they sat, and how John lay in the bosom of the dear Savior. One little fellow looked up with face all aglow, "Mamma, I should like to have been Johnny!" The story, through his imagination, entered his heart and kindled there love for Christ.

Remember that imagination deals only with what is already in the memory. While you are talking the child's imagination is building up the picture as well as it can with what stores it already has. So our words must be simple, child-words all of them.

I once told the Sunday school about David and Goliath, how the lad slew him with a pebble. My little girl's memory had not that word, so she took the one most like it, and told her mother that David slew Goliath, wonderful thing, with a bubble! It takes study and pains to speak clearly to the child imagination. Buy and read to yourself some one-syllable books. Write out a sermon or Sunday school lesson now and then in short words. Most of the inattention of children is caused, I believe, by our long words, meaning nothing to them, and shunting their minds from the track of our thought.

Remember that the child-imagination builds ideals easily. Life's aims are largely directed by these. Hence children need sowing and planting rather than weeding and pruning. Their imaginations apprehend things positively, not negatively; kindle and glow when a holy life is pictured, but shrink timid and discouragedly under cold rebuke. Continual fault-finding discourages them. Nagging and scolding are fatal to child-growth. What a sad picture that is in George Combe's autobiography, where he tells how all his childhood he pined and hungered for that approving, encouraging word which never came. A smile, a kind word, a caress are gentle dew and rain upon the fallow soil of the child-nature. Tell the little ones more about that Savior who will forgive the penitent child seventy times seven times in a day. Tell them about the prodigal's Father. Lead them to Him. Have hope for them, and give them the hopefulness. We are saved by faith. There is no danger of a child having too much faith. Why, by rebukes and discouragement, fill it with doubts and fears?

Child-memory has two characteristics—readiness to acquire and readiness to forget. Hence it should be stored with golden words and thoughts, and they should be often reviewed. A child once taught is not taught forever. After driving we must clinch. I am afraid that we make a great blunder in filling these bright, hungry, but slippery, little memories with a thousand non-essential things, instead of taking more pains to drive home the great truths. Better a few essential truths about God and the Bible and the soul, clearly understood, and made a part of the child's being by reiteration, illustration, explanation and example, than a thousand non-essentials left unexplained in the memory, and which the youth or man may have to give up with shock after shock to his faith. This may be somewhat hard upon denominationalism. It will be good for the child and for Christianity. I would therefore stock the memory with the sweetest and richest and strongest things of the Bible, clearly understood, and fixed there. I would make him love the word of God above his necessary food, and I would leave him to become wiser than all his teachers in minor and disputed matters by his more mature study.

Children are intensely logical. They have that sort of logic which Sir William Hamilton said that Dr. Guthrie had in his sermons—where there is but one step between the premise and the conclusion—the strongest and the best logic it is, Sir William Hamilton said. This should teach us several things.

The child must be brought to a decision for Christ. Drifting in uncertainty is illogical, and the child knows it. "Are you a Christian? Will you be one now and henceforth?" These questions require immediate pressing. This is not exactly "early conversion," for the child may be already a child of God, and need no conversion; but it does need clear, definite choice of Christ in any case. The logic of the child-mind tends to follow out the choice in a growing Christian life.

And the practical logic of child-nature demands that its ideals be made very simple and every-day. Every talk at the mother's knee about Jesus, every Sunday school lesson needs to be made practical. The infant class teacher told the story of the cross and asked, "What will you do for Jesus?" A poor little girl, who was hardly used, and whose weary little bare feet were often reluctant to go where they were bidden, said, "I'll run his arrants." Can't you imagine how that lesson was made practical for her and the rest? We often find it hard for ourselves to make the connection between the boiler and the engine, as Phillips Brooks says, between our warm love and our practical living; we must help the little folks to do this.

Child-logic keenly comprehends the logic of a life. I was once in a reform club meeting, and listened with interest, as all did, until a neighbor drew a half-emptied whisky bottle from the speaker's pocket. Logic was against him, and his words did not count after that. Who can express the importance of the teacher's own piety? Of the parents' and Christian brothers' and sisters' home life? If we talk much about business and pleasure and our neighbors, and little about spiritual things, the child-logic will value them accordingly. If we have our boy give a penny to the heathen, and five cents for candy or fruit, will he not value the gospel and the fruit or candy accordingly? I am persuaded that the small gifts of mature Christians are to be charged in part to the training of their tender years. Children do not readily believe that one is a hypocrite. They sooner place the hypocrite's valuation upon the gospel. The merciless and stern logic of our child demands a holy life of us.

Individuality naturally comes last. "Train up a child in the way he should go—according to his way"—is the Hebrew. We can't make Christians as we do spools and buttons. We have got to know each child and suit our approaches to his needs. I remember how one little boy was urged by his teacher again and again to be converted. Poor little chap, he was loving Jesus and trying to serve Him. He needed encouragement, faith, hope. The exhortations made him feel that something was wrong he knew not what. So he gave the whole thing up in despair, and waited fifteen years for the Lord to convert him. The teacher urged the wrong boy. Soul-medicine must be given intelligently. And remember that children change like that little green shoot of the spring, which is tall and budding in a few months. Your boy of six months ago is not the boy of to-day. While there are many things which may be said to all children, yet there are others which must be fitted to each child's present heart. A quick, intelligent, loving, familiar sympathy with the little one's inner life is essential to success. Close that door to your child's nature by harshness and unreasonableness, and you will never enter that inner life more. We must be children with the children, and win, at any cost of self-pleasing authority and government, the inner citadel of the heart. And so we get back again to what we started with—the affections. Love first and last.

And who is sufficient for these things? You thought when your first-born came that all the difficulty would be in understanding that heart! No. Each new child is a new problem requiring a new solution. O hard and heavy task! I felt what Mr. Moody said Tuesday afternoon, "Ministers do not know how to talk to mothers; it needs a mother to do it." That is true. I wish a mother were in my place to-day. I wish my mother could speak to you to-day. But I rest my faith and hope on Him who loved the little ones; so that they came to His arms and sung His hosannahs.

He loves my little ones, too, my Sunday-school class. I will seek for guidance from that Spirit who was on Him without measure. He is freely given to those who ask Him.

Mr. Sankey then addressed the convention on the topic:

"HOW MAY MUSIC BE BEST USED AND CONTROLLED IN PROMOTING WORSHIP AND SPREADING THE GOSPEL?"

He said:

This is a broad question, covering a good deal of ground. I will not attempt to cover all the ground, but I will make a few statements, the result of years of experience in trying to teach the gospel in song. About thirteen years ago I left my home in Pennsylvania to attend a convention of the Young Men's Christian Association held at Indianapolis. I had been engaged in Christian work for many years, and had been leading a service of praise in my own town. I was sent by the Association to attend the convention at Indianapolis. I remember one morning, at the early hour of six o'clock, a prayer meeting was announced, to be held in the Baptist Church there, to be conducted by my friend who presides at this meeting. My delegation promised to be there. Getting up early, we went there and found the room crowded. The meeting was going on, and an old gentleman, a godly man, was leading the singing. He was singing some of the very old hymns with very old tunes, and the congregation of young men were not singing as they might. I remember a Rev. Mr. McMullen was sitting by me, and during a prayer, he asked me at the conclusion to sing one of the gospel hymns.

I did not like to interfere, but he said it was a young men's meeting, and the young men were not taking the interest they would if the music were such as they could and would sing. I started one of the hymns I knew they were all accustomed to singing. We sang, "There is a fountain filled with blood." I remember how the young men there took hold of that hymn and such a volume as rose upon the air. That morning was the first time I ever met our brother here. We met in that prayer meeting, and have been together almost ever since. I remember that twelve years ago I came to this city at his invitation, and the day I arrived we went to visit a number of poor families on the North Side. We went into these poor homes, among the sick and the dying, and Mr. Moody would pray with the people and ask me to sing a hymn. The hearts of these people were touched and they were bound to Christ, I believe that the work of that day will tell in eternity. I believe God blessed that day's work. Then in the winter after the fire we worked among these poor people and God blessed our efforts. I believe He blessed these gospel hymns, and gave them a power that they never had before.

When we were in Glasgow a poor mother came up to me and said, "I want to tell you about my little Mary. She was struck by the gospel hymns, and especially by the one. 'Safe in the arms of Jesus.' The child loved the hymn and was always singing it. Six months ago little Mary sickened and died, but just before she died she said, 'Mother, raise me up, and get my hymn-book, and find No. 12.' That was her favorite, and she sang it through, and as I laid her down again she said, 'Mother, I am going now to be with Jesus. Please lay my little hymn-book in the coffin on my breast open at that page.'"

And so little Mary died singing "Safe in the arms of Jesus," and was laid away with that hymn in her grave. There are so many of these little incidents that I have no question that God has blessed these hymns, and they have been a blessing to the people.

Very much depends upon the minister of the gospel in the singing in church, as to whether it shall prove effective or not. I feel the importance of this, that the church should take charge of the music and conduct it, and not let the choir take it and do as they please. I find that there are two parties in the church often, and there is a difference of opinion as to conducting the services. I think, though, all services should be conducted by the minister. When the leaders have not good voices to lead, the church should take charge and appoint those who will. I find that with very little leading the people will sing well, and think that has been pretty well demonstrated here to-day. There should be a good supply of books in the pews. I agree with what Mr. Jacobs said this morning about Bibles in the churches, but I also want plenty of hymn-books. It is hard for the people to worship God without hymn-books. The churches, many of them, most of them, have too large and too expensive books. If they would have smaller books and larger collections of them, so that there would be books for all strangers who come in, it would result in better singing.

Another point is regarding the organ. It should be in front, near the pulpit. I would have the singers in front also. I should have as many in the choir as possible, but they should all be Christian singers to lead in the songs of praise. [Applause].

When we went to England we made a point of this. We sent word to the places where we were to hold meetings that we wanted Christian choirs. You know whether God blessed that work. God was with the singers. I have noticed that so far as we have departed from that rule we have not had the good results. We have had excellent singing from choirs, but while the song was grand there was not that spiritual power manifest when we had Christians in the choir.

As to the organ-playing, I believe in teaching the sons and daughters to play. I have a son learning to play church music, and I would rather have been a good player on the organ than a finished pianist. If we had several in the Church who could play the organ and be ready to take the organist's place, we might not have so much trouble with him. It would have a good effect to say to him once in a while that his place could be supplied if he did not like to play the music the church wanted. If I could not get a Christian choir, I believe I should go back to the old form in Scotland and have a precentor—have a man stand up before the congregation and invite the people to sing. That kind of singing will get the congregation to singing better. Then there is solo singing. I would use it sparely, but I would use it. If I had one who had a voice and heart to sing I should let him or her sing, but it must be from the heart. I believe David sung solos ; but I never sung a solo in my life to worship God. I have sung little songs that had a story which I wished to give to the people.

Mr. Sankey then told the story of meeting an old Scotchman on board a steamer when crossing to Europe, and when they sang some of the gospel hymns, he thought it was a sin to worship God with songs composed by human beings. He wanted the psalms sung. When that man heard the "Ninety and Nine" sung he wept like a child and wanted the whole collection, and invited the singer to visit him and sing them to his family. That man's prejudices were broken down by a simple story in song. There was solo singing, congregational singing, artistic singing, and evangelical singing. In regard to the last, he believed in explaining the hymns and getting the people to thoroughly understand them before letting them sing. Mr. Spurgeon always talked over his hymns until the people were fired with them and and all aglow with enthusiasm to sing.

I think that if some ministers would make more of music it would be better. Mr. Moody makes a good deal of singing; but I think we might have more of it. If you give it to children you will get their help. And so in regard to the matter of singing; if you take hold of it you can make it a power. It will be a power if you seek to make it so. But I would not like to have it frittered away. I think the church ought to manage it—have charge of it.

Now, are there any questions you would like to ask? If so, I will try my best to answer them.

The following questions and answers were then asked and given:

"What do you think of interludes?"

I would have a very simple interlude; possibly the concluding strain of a hymn, perhaps the concluding strain of the hymn you have just been singing; but you may have an improvised interlude just to give the singers a rest. I do not like the instruments. The melody is broken thereby. It is like a break in a prayer meeting when nobody comes up to pray. The value of the interlude is that the instrument keeps up the tune in which you have been singing. I think there can be no objection to that. But the interlude that is interjected sometimes between the verses, that have nothing in them in the spirit of the singing, I think is all wrong. I was quite interested once in a church where I was with my family. After the services a little boy said to his mother: "Mamma, the tune that that lady played to was the tune that was played in Barnum's procession." It really was that tune. It was a popular tune, and the lady played it as we went out. Even the little boy, with his quick ear, recognized it."

"How about the case of cornets and other musical instruments in connection with the organ?"

That question was asked me in private by a minister on the platform. I said, "yes;" that there could be no objection to their introduction if it was done by a body of Christian young men—distinctively Christian men. If they were such I would like them to use them, if they wished. They had them or similar instruments in old times—organs and cymbals and timbrels. I don't see if we have them why we should not use them and have the best music we can; though I don't think I would have them used in regular church services. But in evangelical services, I would use them, and use them in a Christian manner."

"Would you go out of church collections for hymns?"

No sir; I think there are plenty of beautiful hymns in our church collections.

"What do you think of the introduction of classical music?"

I will tell you in regard to that. At one place in England where we had four services a day, being tired, I went out and went to a cathedral in the city, as it was said that at a certain time every day, four o'clock, there was a beautiful singing service—classic music—by the best singers in England. It was true. I went there, supposing that I would hardly be able to get in, though it was a very large cathedral. There were about fifty singers, and I believe I never heard sweeter singing or more beautiful music. I sat down and looked around for the congregation, but I saw none. Soon I was lulled to a sense of sweet, melodious music. Again I looked around to see how many had arrived and were listening to the music. Just fourteen—a service that had cost several hundred dollars for that afternoon alone; only fourteen persons to enjoy that splendid music.

"Don't you think that circus songs can be converted into church music?"

No. I don't think I would go out and get the circus tunes.

"What if the circus tunes become circumcised?" asked a humorous minister.

Mr. Sankey, answering: "Perhaps it might do them good."

"Do you think it right to pay singers for their services?"

I have no objection to those who devote their lives to singing being paid. The laborer is worthy of his hire. But I think you can find enough singers in the congregation who will do it for nothing; but the leader should be paid.

Answers were then given as follows to questions put:

I would have a choir and I would have more of its singing in the church before the preaching commences. If you did this you would get more practice and the result also would be larger congregations. I think the tendency is to have too monotonous forms in singing. We have had the same hymns sung here in half a dozen different forms. I do not know, however, that I would have that in regular services."

"What do you think about music after services are closed?"

I would not have any playing after benediction is pronounced. Mr. Spurgeon, when he closes his addresses, raises his hand and pronounces the benediction, and they go away filled with the truth and talking about it. They do not have the music to dispel the service from their minds. I liked the method very much. They went away filled with his service. I don't like the singing to come in to drive away the gospel. I don't like the church to become a singing-school.

At this point some "unsankeymonious" infidel in the audience called out:

"Will you please sing us '99' to break this monotony."

Mr. Sankey good naturedly responded:

Yes, after I get through. I would advise the Sabbath school to use such hymns as can be used in the church; and I would have a children's hymn too. I think I would have a special hymn for them. I would also have such hymns in the Sunday school as would induce them to read good gospel truth. In the evening services I would have gospel hymns sung, though using the regular hymn book in the morning services.

"What do you think of singing in parts?"

I would have lead the whole four parts. In Germany, where they have the best congregational singing in the world, they all sing the same part. I think it is nice for the quartet to sing alone; then the congregation sing a portion. What can be objected to it? I think breaking up the monotony by going from one part to congregational singing is not a bad thing.

"Why cannot we have a singing union of Sunday school scholars in Chicago as well as they have in London?"

There is no reason why we cannot; but I think the project of Mr. Moody for a training school for Bible readers, colporteurs, home missionaries, etc., would, perhaps, be the best. I think this training school should have one department for training people how to take charge of singing in the Sunday school. It is easy to criticise a singer who conducts Sunday school exercises, but where can they get trained men? They are prepared in regular colleges or otherwise for singing in concerts, but there is no place where Christian singers can be taught their duties. I hope we will have a branch of this sort. [Applause.]

Mr. Sankey having taken, as he thought, sufficient time in the fruitful process of answering these pertinent questions on church music, Mr. James McGranahan was introduced and continued the subject. Propounding the topical question.

Mr. McGranahan said: First (negatively), it cannot be best used and controlled in promoting worship by those who are not worshipers. "God is a Spirit, and those who worship Him must worship Him in spirit and in truth." It cannot be best used and controlled for spreading the gospel by those who do not believe and receive the gospel; by those who have not tasted and seen that the Lord is good; who have not quenched their own thirst by drinking of the water of life; who have not received Christ, and with Him the gift of eternal life.

By education and culture a Pharisee may frame what to human ear may seem a beautiful, well-rounded prayer, and yet be like the one who stood in the temple, and prayed thus with himself; "God, I thank Thee, I am not as other men. I fast, I give of all I possess." It is the I, I, I, I, I, five times in a single breath: he has no need of the Spirit to help his infirmities; he is praying "with himself," while the poor Publican, you remember, could not so much as lift up his eyes, for he was not praying "with himself," but to God, and as he prayed with the spirit "God be merciful to me, a sinner," we are told he "went down to his house justified."

And just so may it be with the singer; by his art he may sing the precious truths of the gospel with such careful expression and studied effect that to human ear, there is, perhaps, nothing more to desire, and yet if he has never bowed to the truth he sings, God knows it is all art and not heart, and like the praying of the Pharisee, it is more with himself than with the spirit of God.

Come with me into the studio of the sculptor; see that piece of statuary—beautiful, true to nature—faithfully fashioned in every

LIBRARY
OF THE
UNIVERSITY OF ILLINOIS

feature to "human form divine," as a work of art, it is a triumph, but as a thing of life, it is cold and inanimate as the quarry from whence it was taken. It is nothing more than was Adam before God breathed into his nostrils the breath of life, and he became a living soul. Life-like as it may seem, who would send it to Washington to represent them in Congress, or the Senate Chamber, or, if they did, would the President mistake it for a Senator—he might give it a place in his Cabinet—but it would be among his geological specimens, and not his counselors.

Come, now, into one of our well-ordered (?) fashionable churches. It is the morning service, and the exercises have just commenced. What a grand organ; brilliant organist, and the choir superb, soprano so clear, alto so rich, tenor so tender, bass so deep, and the music so delightful! Nothing better outside of the concert-room or behind the footlights. Isn't it fine? Well, suppose it is; so is the statuary in the studio.

But how about the worship? Do they believe what they sing? Are they Christians? They do not even profess to be. They sing because they love to sing, or, perhaps, they regard the church as a harmless, respectable sort of institution, and kindly favor it with their patronage, or, as a mere matter of business, sing because they are paid for it. But, in the light of God's word, can the music under such circumstances be regarded as in any degree calculated to promote the worship of God or the spread of the gospel. As well might we expect a graven image to render acceptable service to the President at Washington as the singer who is still dead in trespasses and sins, not having been "born again," to render acceptable worship to the King of kings and Lord of lords.

When the sculptor, with his chisel, can put the breath of life into his marble statue and make it a living soul to fitly represent a living people, then perhaps the singer who is spiritually dead may hope to breathe into his song spiritual life and power such as shall promote the worship of God and the spread of the gospel.

But the sculptor does not claim life for his statue, but only a likeness to life—an imitation of that which has life—a specimen of his workmanship in the art of sculpture. And can more be claimed for the music of the sanctuary when thus produced by those who are, in the language of the Scripture, "dead in trespasses and sin?"

Would it not be in entire conformity with the truth sometimes, if the minister, instead of saying, "Let us continue the worship of God by singing to His praise," a certain psalm or hymn, if he should put it in some such way as this: "We will now suspend the worship of God for a short time and listen to some music from the choir, who will kindly give us a devotional selection in imitation of the worship of God, that which has real musical merit, and will at the same time show off the voices to good advantage, that the congregation may see that they are getting what they subscribed for, viz., good music!"

"But," says one, "do you object to good music in church services?" I answer, "far from it." Let us have music fitting and appropriate and the best of its kind; but when it is the mere rendering of good music for its own sake, a musical performance of whatever merit, call it by its right name—an entertainment, a concert, anything you deem proper—but do not miscall it worship. To expect spiritual power or blessing from such a service of song would be like expecting a well-drilled army to defend our city against the invasion of a mighty enemy without either bullet or ball. If noise and smoke were all that were necessary, then powder and blank cartridges might be sufficient; but since it is not the thunder of the guns that does the execution but the shot and shell through them, so it is not the voices nor the music, but the spirit of God through them, that carries conviction with the truth that is sung. That music has power is not called in question. Who has listened to the strains of the old masters and not felt it? What can be more impressive, at least to the musician's ear, than the wonderful harmonies that Handel has used in some of his grand oratorio choruses. For instance, the closing of "All We Like Sheep," where the harmonies breathe forth so impressively the sad but life-giving message, "And the Lord hath laid on Him the iniquity of us all." It seems to me no one can listen to it and not be moved; and yet if they have no interest in the divine message it bears, but are simply moved by "the concord of sweet sounds," its power is as fleeting as the passing clouds and its effect vanishes as the morning dew before the summer sun. He listens and weeps and goes on as before in his selfish pursuit of pleasure and sin, regardless of God and the Savior He hath given.

I remember on a certain occasion a musical director of some distinction, in speaking of the power of music apart from and independent of words, made reference to the "Hallelujah Chorus" in this way: "The choir begins with 'Hallelujah, hallelujah, hallelujah;' and then sings 'Hallelujah, hallelujah,' after which they proceed to sing 'Hallelujah, hallelujah,' etc., nothing but hallelujah, while the music keeps building up higher and grander at every repetition of the word." Now, at first thought, and perhaps to many a mind, it may have seemed like a meaningless jingle of syllables thrown in merely to accommodate the music, but when we take into account the meaning of this word "Hallelujah"—"Praise Jehovah," then we have the sequel to its multiplied repetitions. It is hallelujah, hallelujah, page after page, with music among the grandest that has ever been written. And what is all this "hallelujah" about, the closing pages reveal it, "For the Lord God Omnipotent reigneth." We shall comprehend it better when His kingdom has come, when He shall have appeared, when we shall be like Him and see Him as He is. It was the mighty power of this inspired message finding fit utterance through the music, that brought that royal audience to its feet on the occasion of its first rehearsal, and ever since in every land, it is the custom for the audience, Christian and infidel, to reverently stand during the singing of the "Hallelujah Chorus."

Music as a performance is one thing, and its use in divine worship is another. Its power in worship is only manifest when it has its proper place and relation to the worshipers, and becomes a simple medium through which is poured forth, from hearts that know the "joy of salvation" praise, prayer or adoration to Him whose they are; or a means of expressing or enforcing the truths of the psalm or hymn; and thus, if you please, it is simply an emphatic way of preaching.

What speech is to the intellect song is to the heart.

The minister in the pulpit reads the psalm or hymn, and so far as the power of speech may go he brings out the truth thereof. Then the worshipers, with the voice of united song, take it up as the language of their own hearts, and pour forth their praises to Him who alone is worthy. And as the Spirit, according to His promise, guides into the truth and fills each heart with a sense of its reality, then is made manifest the power and blessing of the "service of song."

2. That the service of song may be effective we must, as in I. Corinthians, xiv., 7, "Sing with the understanding." "Even things without life-giving sound, except they give a distinction in the sounds, how shall it be known what is piper or harper?" If these things without life are to be clearly intelligible how much more should living human voices be understood. Paul says, "Let him that speaketh in an unknown tongue pray that he may interpret;" and just so in singing. If the choir sing in an unknown tongue let them have an interpreter, but if they sing in their own vernacular let them so sing that there shall be no need of one.

Again he says (I Cor. xiv., 14), "If I pray in an unknown tongue, my spirit prayeth but my understanding is unfruitful." Illustrations of this are not uncommon in the prayer-meeting where some one in a distant part of the room undertakes to lead in a tone too feeble to be intelligible to those around him. While he may be praying with the spirit, he is become a barbarian to those who would join with him. Again (15th verse), "I will pray with the spirit and I will pray with the understanding also; I will sing (in the same way) with the spirit and I will sing with the understanding also."

In my native town lives an old man now, who is always in his pew on the Sabbath, and no matter what the tune—new or old, high or low, loud or soft, he is always ready with his part, for it is always the same, and no matter whether there be scores or hundreds—like the bass note of an organ when the key sticks—it may always be heard. While, no doubt, his spirit sings, his understanding can hardly be said to be fruitful, at least so far as others are concerned. Paul plainly means that if we have voices, and the use of our powers, we are responsible for using them to the edification of others. And as we see how God is using the singing of the gospel in these days to reach men's hearts, it ought to stimulate us to a more general education in this direction, until the ability to read the music would be as common as to read the hymns. Why not?

3. To sing with the understanding I must be clear on two points: First, is what I sing true? and second, am I true in singing it? First, is what I sing true? Perhaps one of the greatest hindrances to power in the "service of song" lies in the fact that in the vast number of hymns that have been written, some have found their way into use (more or less) that are simply the production of human wisdom or fancy, and when brought under the light of God's word are found to be but chaff. They may be good sentiment and have poetic flow, but if they do not contain the everlasting truth of God's word, power or blessing can not flow from them. It is the Spirit's office to take of the things that are Christ's and show them unto us; but if there be nothing of His in it, what has the spirit to do? We have no promise of blessing on that which stands only in the wisdom of man, apart from the wisdom of God, for man's wisdom is foolishness in His sight. As it is written, "He that hath a dream, let him tell his dream, but he that hath my word, let him speak it faithfully; for what is the chaff to the wheat, saith the Lord." If we want power we must not sing dreams, but the pure wheat of the gospel, according to the word of God!

Second, if what I sing is true, am I true in singing it? It is not enough to sing the truth, but we must stand where we can make it the sincere language of our own hearts. Not long since I overheard a friend of mine ask a man—a church member—the question, "Are you saved?" To which he calmly replied: "It is a very solemn thing, sir, for any man this side of the grave to say he is saved." "Yes," said my friend, "It would be a solemn thing for any man to say he had a thousand dollars in his pocket if he did not have; but if he did have it would quite alter the case." And yet from childhood, I doubt not, this canny Scotchman had been singing.

> "The Lord's my shepherd, I'll not want,
>   He makes me down to lie
> In pastures green, he leadeth me
>   The quiet waters by.

> "Goodness and mercy all my life
> Shall surely follow me,
> And God's house forevermore
> My dwelling place shall be."

And what precious truth this is, and with what power and blessing it comes to the trusting child of God. But suppose you just ask this man the question: "Is it true that the Lord is your shepherd? Is it true that God's house is to be your dwelling-place forevermore?" I think I hear him answer, "It is a solemn thing, sir,' for any man this side the grave to say that." And so it is, if he do not say it truthfully, and though he may sing it with the voice of a Brignoli, a Sims Reeves, a Whitney, aye, or angel from heaven, if he be not true in singing it, it can have no power except it be to condemn. How, then, can we expect blessing to flow from those who, when thus singing, are changing the precious truth into a lie upon their lips?

But says one, what shall we do? Must we stop singing?"

In the first place, if the truth condemns, be honest, accept the situation and turn to God by an earnest, unconditional surrender to His Son as your Savior, for "There is no condemnation to them that are in Christ Jesus." And then, being on the side of truth, when you sing it will not only bring blessing to your own soul, but to those who hear. I remember an instance of a lady in Dundee, Scotland, that will illustrate. We were all singing the hymn:

> "I've found a friend, O, such a friend,
>   He loved me ere I knew Him.
> He drew me with the cords of love,
>   And thus he bound me to Him.
> And round my heart still closely twine
>   Those ties, which naught can sever,
> For I am His and He is mine,
>   Forever and forever."

And as she sung along, the thought stole over her that she was dishonest in singing such utterances; that although she knew about Jesus she never had accepted Him as her Savior and friend, and that the language of her own lips condemned her, and right there she accepted the situation that she was condemned and that Jesus was the only friend that could help her, and before leaving the room that night she did surrender to him and became one of the most successful and earnest workers in the inquiry meetings. Then she could sing "I've found a friend," and be true in singing it. And so, fellow-singer, I would say to thee, don't stop singing, but "Go thou and do likewise;" surrender to Christ; accept Him as your Savior and Redeemer and then on redemption ground you can sing with the Psalmist, and be true in singing:

> "He took me from a fearful pit
> And from the miry clay,
> And on a rock he set my feet.
> Establishing my way.
>
> "He put a new song in my mouth,
> Our God to magnify."

I know of nothing so well calculated to promote the worship of God as to get this new song in the heart:

> "He put a new song in my mouth,
> Our God to magnify."

And the result will be that

> "Many shall see it and shall fear,
> And on the Lord rely."

To have the new song in the heart is to be a new creature in Christ Jesus. Then old things pass away. All things become new. A lady once read a book recommended by a friend, but was somewhat disappointed in finding it less interesting than she anticipated; but later she made the acquaintance of its author. She admired him. She grew to love him, and he won her heart. On returning to the book again she was amazed at her former stupidity in failing to discover the beauty and charm that now seemed to glitter upon every page. It was a new book to her. It was written by the one who had won her heart. So, the simple gospel song that was once so uninteresting, so meager, and almost empty, becomes a new thing, full of sweetness and charm when we wake up to the discovery that it tells the story of His love, who laid down His life that He might win us to Himself; that He might make us His bride. I never listen to the grand oratorios of the old masters but I am seized with a desire to wield such harmonies for the glory of my Master, for the "new song" in the heart is so grandly sublime, and my poor pen so feeble and inadequate. And then I think, perhaps if I could do so, it would defeat the very object of my desire and only lead the hearer to exclaim, "Oh, what music!" instead of, "Oh, what a Savior!"

We are told of a great painter who once undertook to represent the scene of Jesus with His disciples as they were assembled around the supper-table for the last time. He had summoned all his powers as an artist to depict the heavenly visage of the divine and central One. The work was completed; a group of admiring friends were gazing on the picture. One of them called attention to the exquisite beauty of the cups and vessels on the table, when to their astonishment the artist with one sweep of his brush blotted them out of the picture. The form of the Savior was to be the focal point—the central figure, and anything that would interfere with that idea was out of proportion, and a blemish so serious that it could not be tolerated; and so it is with the "new song." Jesus is the focal point, the central figure, and the music that recognizes this and keeps Him there, is the music that will best promote the worship of God and the spread of the gospel. And the music that does not put the truth in the foreground, but by its beauty, its excellence, its grandeur or its anything else, takes the central place for itself, if we are true to our Master as the painter was to his art, in the name of the Master what shall we do with it?

When Mr. McGranahan had finished his paper, which was well received by the audience, Mr. Moody remarked that the Question Drawer had been omitted from the programme that the subject of church music might be the better ventilated. Having requested the singing of two hymns, one, "Jesus Shall Reign," to the grand music of "The Watch on the Rhine," and the other, "Am I a Soldier of the Cross?"

Mr. Moody himself had something to say on the important topic still presented to the brethren for further discussion. He said that he knew it was a delicate subject, but that he thought the time had come to speak out. He wondered that a man, such as Mr. Morton on the previous day had mentioned, could know any fear and trembling before getting up to address an audience. For his own part Mr. Moody never had a feeling of this kind for such a reason, but when it came to hearing back of him one of those high-toned choirs singing an unknown tune, then came a time when he was really embarrassed. He had once occupied a pulpit when he gave out a hymn that he felt sure they couldn't set a strange tune to; they surely wouldn't find something new for "Jesus, Lover of My Soul," but they did.

In Boston not long since Mr. Moody was attending one of its most prominent churches, only to be distressed throughout the entire service by seeing the organist, when he desisted from his performance, take up a Sunday newspaper, and read to within five minutes of the close of the sermon. By such conduct and spirit a minister was fettered in his work. Wasn't it time to speak out, exclaimed Mr. Moody. There might be one in every twenty-five or fifty who wanted the music that he abominated, but the congregations, as a whole, wanted something they could understand, and their numbers were diminishing because they couldn't get it. If anybody advocated the use of that kind of a choir that embarrassed him let him speak out. Some one on the platform suggesting that perhaps there might be more profit in reading a newspaper than in listening to some preachers, Mr. Moody warmly retorted that he didn't think a Christian man ought to read Sunday newspapers. An old man in the audience spoke up and asked if one couldn't ride in the horse-cars on Sunday. "No," tersely rejoined Mr. Moody: "you don't want to take their Sunday away from somebody else."

Mr. Moody also seemed to hold strong views on the propriety of Sunday railroad travelling.

Shortly he called upon Major Whittle, for the soul of both of them was in this subject, and the latter advanced and said that he would as soon have an unconverted preacher to preach as an unconverted singer to sing. He held that it must be abominable in the sight of God. He strengthened his assertion by affirming that whenever there came a revival in the church the singing was always on the part of the people and God blessed the work. What power, he reminded his hearers, had there been in Mr. Bliss, with whom he went forth to preach Christ, when he sat down by the organ and sang God's truth Major Whittle had sat in Spurgeon's vast tabernacle, where 5,000 people united in praising God, and there he had felt himself nearer Heaven than in any other place on earth.

But the day was drawing to its close. So Mr. Moody, doubtless with his soul refreshed by the timely words of his clerical lieutenants, asked the singing by Mr. Sankey of the dear old "Ninety and Nine."

Mr. Sankey complied. But first, as is much his wont, he spoke a few words of earnest prayer that help might be his when soon he should sing the song across the waters, in the land where it was written. Then asking that there might be loyalty in the hearts of all who sang in the service of Christ, this big, tender man of simple song, probably for the last time in Chicago for many a day, sang, amid the silence that moves by its silence, the verses of the touching gospel hymn,

> 'There were ninety and nine that safely lay
> In the shelter of the fold."

Rev. Dr. Henson, of the First Baptist Church, rose, after the singing, and said:

I do not believe in a pulpit performance and I do not believe in a choir performance in a church. There are plenty of places to perform in without going into the house of God. A church is not for performances, but for work; and I believe that the minister is responsible for the character of these services of song, and not the choir. I believe if a minister cannot control the character of the singing in his church, and keep it in Christian hands and in Christian ways, he is not fit for a minister, and had better abdicate. [Laughter and applause.] I believe ministers are consecrated for the regulation of the services of God's house, and that the singing is a part of that service. I remember going once to New York, to preach for a church that had no pastor. Before I went the leader of the music in the church sent me a note saying that I need not bother myself about the selection of music for the service I was to conduct. I sent him word that if he would come down to see me I would adapt my sermon to his music. And he came down—in more senses than one. [Laughter.] I have heard here soloists that lifted me up to the very throne of God. I have heard a quartet that made my soul respond to the soul of the music. I believe in such music as that. [Applause.]

Dr. Herrick Johnson then rose and said:

And yet there is a word to be said about that. I know a preacher who did not know the difference between an opera tune and "Old Hundred." [Laughter.] No doubt this charge of the singing in a church ought to be in somebody's hands who has intelligence in the matter, and who will see that it shall be made such a part of the worship as it ought to be in a Christian church; just as much a part of the service as the prayer—and a song is a prayer when properly voiced, as it is in many of our homes. I believe in a quartet choir, and in a trained choir, and I believe in time we shall have them all over the country as we have them here in Chicago. I hope we shall always have true church singing—singing from the heart; music that makes melody in our hearts and souls. Now, in reference to what we shall sing! We want hymn-books that may be used by all. Songs should be sensible, and they should not be unscriptural. I have seen songs in song books that were neither sensible nor Scriptural—songs that express a state of quiescence simply, with no activity, no high service for God, and we ought not to be set to singing those.

The exercises of the afternoon were concluded by Dr. Kennard, who pronounced the benediction.

EVENING SESSION.

It is no use piling up adjectives in reference to the crowd that tried to get into Farwell Hall this last night to get a last glimpse of Mr. Moody and hear the last words that that great leader of the people should utter before he should leave Chicago. It will give one some idea of the jam that took place to say that many people did not leave the hall, and at 6 o'clock there were 1,000 people on the sidewalk waiting patiently until the policemen at the door should say they might pass into the hall. No sooner were the doors opened than the hall was filled in every part, and the people packed in a manner that would have disgusted sardines. Even the stairways were crowded, although there was no more hope of hearing a word said in the hall above than there was getting into that hall. The speakers who came late had to be lifted over the crowd that choked up the entrance. As for the members of the press who found themselves detailed to report the meeting, after their experience in passing through that crowd no one would wonder that they could pass through key-holes after secrets. It would in theory be easier to pass through the eye of a needle than gain admission to the hall through the crowd last night.

As the people were there and must remain it was concluded to open the meeting nearly an hour earlier than announced, and at 7:10 o'clock Mr. Moody appeared and announced a hymn, which was sung with enthusiasm. Mr. Morehead made the opening prayer, and Dr. Goodwin followed him in a stirring speech, urging that the people consecrate themselves to the work. He spoke of his recent sojourn in California, and the work he had undertaken since his return. He believed that every man should present himself for such work as the Lord would have him to do.

Mr. William Reynolds, of Peoria, followed Dr. Goodwin, and after a prayer by the Rev. Mr. Williams, Professor Morehead and Mr. Lattimer made short speeches.

Dr. Hatfield took the stand to perpetuate the spirit of the evening. He said that the three days past had been days of special interest, red-letter days in the lives of the many present. It all reminded him of a scene described in the holy book, the scene of the transfiguration, when Peter said, "Let us make three tabernacles." He would have all stay there permanently. So, continued the speaker, would the people who had attended the expiring convention look back and wish that they might continue to dwell together. Yet it might be that all had lingered long enough in the place of transfiguration, so let the people go forth into the field and take up the work.

The speaker kindly and wisely bade no one be unhappy that he or she could not do just what, or in the very way, that some one else did, something for the cause. For each there was a mission. The great thing was to be found honest and faithful in work. For fidelity of service were the rewards at the last day meted out. Some one had said (Johnson, thought the speaker), that if two of the chiefest angels in all heaven were to descend to earth, one to be a prime minister of a State and the other to sweep the streets of its capital, with them there would be known no difference in vocation, whether this was the office of minister and the other that of scavenger.

To these servants of God there was no precedence. The sweeping of a room might, in the very nature of the action, be made divine. To glorify God as did the great sun was a grand thing, but it was no mean thing to be as the little star that shone in the firmament above. The mighty ocean was grand, but the little brook had its place as well. There were no small things in God's cause.

The speaker bade his hearers when they departed to their homes to go with stout, brave, Christian hearts. Much had Dr. Hatfield and all heard about testimony, but the former had in his mind an instance of testimony that was the most affecting he had ever heard. And this testimony was the testimony of a poor deaf and dumb girl who, at a camp meeting, in the sight of all, testified mutely, with her simple gestures, that her heart was God's. Very much like a camp meeting, resumed the speaker, was the convention, though, he jocosely added to the amusement of many, all the brethren could not appreciate the fact. Dr. Hatfield continued in saying that he had noticed that at times of revival, men who had been impressed and yet turned away, were in a worse condition than before; and this seemed to be in recognition of a mental law that truth not acted upon became a curse. If good resolutions were to be their own end, then those who had come and made them had been better off to have remained away.

He charged his hearers to see that their resolutions were followed up, that they might not be like men looking into a glass and then going away to forget what manner of men they were. Revealing in himself the liberal, undenominational spirit that seemed to pervade the whole convention, Dr. Hatfield declared that if he and his associated brethren proved themselves bigoted and narrow-spirited after all that had passed, they would all desire to be tumbled neck and heels out of the fraternity. Pleasantly confessing that the barriers seemed so thoroughly burned away that he couldn't distinguish the Methodist brethren from the others, this man of God, of hard sense and hardihood, with all his heart, quoted Bunyan, who puts into the mouth of some one in his Christian narrative the remark that Mr. Prejudice had fallen and broken his leg, but that it would have been better if he had broken his neck.

Mr. Moody then called on Mr. J. S. Smithson.

Mr. Smithson began his talk by a reference to Christ's meeting with the fishermen, and like their work ours was to be fishers. In the first place we must clean nets, and it was not necessary for us to be great speakers to become great workers in the Lord's cause. A French surgeon being once asked how many operations of a difficult and peculiar kind he had performed, replied 300, but while they were very brilliant, not one had been successful. An English surgeon who had questioned him, said that he had had eight operations of the same kind, and all but one had been successful. With the Christian worker it should be as it had been with the English surgeon, and while we might not be brilliant, we might be successful in what we undertook. It was not brilliant operations and big heads, but with right hearts that we should work. What we wanted was downright hard work. Some said, it was not their sphere to work this or that way. To those he said, do not be waiting for a sphere. You must work where God found you. Some said they could not see any success in the work ahead. That was not the way to look at it, but go to work. The business man did not go around and show his balance sheet and tell his clerks how much he had lost or gained. Do your part, and you may be doing a part that may contribute to the great victory, as much as the clerks contributed to the general result of their employer's business.

The fishermen of the Scripture did not quarrel about who was to catch the biggest fish. They just filled the boats. That was what must be done in the churches. Many had heard the story of the ragged boy with his crooked pin catching fish right under the nose of the gentlemen with fancy rods. It was not brilliant equipment that always caught the fish. Launch out. He remembered that in Dublin they started out to work. Some fear was felt that it would be dangerous and that perhaps there would be trouble. The work was started, and a round of the lodging houses made, and invitations given to the lodgers to come to a breakfast. They elbowed each other, and smiled. They came, and in time those meetings were soon attended by 1,000 Catholics and 500 others. Start out, and go to work. All remembered the story of the great artist who asked for the piece of rough marble, and how out of it he carved the most beautiful figure of an angel. Right here in Chicago there were plenty of pieces of rough marble, out of which might be carved angels. If you thought you were nothing, do not let that hinder you, but remember that in your work is Christ. All know that some had the trick of picking fish from others.

There was in England a class who steal in this way, and are known as poachers. There were some ecclesiastical poachers. That was a very mean trade. Work earnestly in the best way you know. No man ever lost anything by his religion. He never knew a business man who yet lost anything by attending to the Lord's work. There was many a fort to take, and like the volunteers in the Crimean war who marched forward to take a certain fort, we must march out right in our own city and assail the enemy. We could fell the giants of iniquity, though we were but striplings, if we had but faith to trust in God.

MR. MOODY'S CLOSING ADDRESS.

Mr. Moody said that in '76, when the meetings were held in this city, one of the ministers made a remark that had remained with him ever since. They were speaking about the text. "I will pour out waters upon those who are thirsty," and Dr. Gibson said he would like to find the thirsty in his congregation that he might pour out upon them the water. He had thought a good way to find the thirsty would be to carry a bucket of water down the aisle, and those that were thirsty would drink. If the buckets were empty we could not tell who were thirsty. He had thought that himself and other ministers were carrying empty buckets. Was it not true that they were working without having been anointed, without the power for service? The influence of this convention would be lost within thirty days unless they could get power from on high. A colony had gone to Africa, and when they would have settled in one place the natives told them there was one season when it never rained there, and they moved on. In another place they were discouraged in the same manner. But at the third place, the natives said the clouds were pierced, and they settled there. These Christian workers should go under the pierced clouds and then their buckets would always be filled. They could then give of the waters to those who were thirsty and the buckets never be empty. It was so easy to work when we were always filled.

A friend of his living over in Michigan, near the lake, had pipes laid from the lake to his house so that he could draw off the water by simply turning a faucet.

He said it was better than having Lake Michigan, for if he had the whole lake he would not know what to do with it. With the connecting pipe he could draw off just as much of the lake as he wanted and always have a plenty. It was easy to go to a throne of grace and be always filled. Mr. Moody said he had been approached during the afternoon by a man who said he had received a blessing at the meetings held here seven years ago that lasted him ever since. And the speaker believed that such blessings should go out from this meeting. In Birmingham one kind-hearted gentleman had established morning schools for the workingmen. When Mr. Moody was in the place he thought he would look into it. He found that several years ago this gentleman thought he might do something for the workmen of the place, and he tried to establish a school for Sunday mornings. He got up at 7 o'clock and went about carrying out his plans, but it was discouraging, for 7 o'clock was before daylight in the winter mornings, and on Sundays the workmen could not be got up until about 10 o'clock. But he was not discouraged, and kept at his work, until now in Birmingham on Sunday morning one could hear the tramp of these workmen as they went to their school. There were 8,000 men gathered into this morning school and the Christian teachers were there from all over the city to instruct them. It was a grand sight to see this school, and when Mr. Moody visited it he found the Mayor of the city there at that early hour teaching a class of men.

And the influence had not stopped there A lady had been converted and her whole family. There was one member of this family, a gentleman of influence at court, a man of wealth, and in looking about for something to do for the Lord, he thought of the boys. He went down to the "Seven Dials," one of the very worst places in London, and he gathered the boys up that he could persuade to go with him. He gave them their supper, kept them at night, and gave them their breakfast. He then promised to give every one that remained with him a new suit of clothes and find him a place. The boys remained, and night after night he went down to that vile part of the city at 2 o'clock at night, or later, and each time gathered up several of these boys. This was not only for one night, but for every night, and he kept it up for years. And now, as the result of this work, he had a great training school with 2,500 boys and young men, ranging from 17 to 25 years of age, who were learning the trades. It did not mean much being free in this country, but in Europe it did mean a good deal.

Mr. Moody hoped the spirit of the Most High would fall upon this convention and that it would bear good fruit. He hoped that many would go into the vineyard and ask God to teach them what was their work. He had never advised any man to go into the ministry.

It was too high a calling. He had never advised any man to go into the foreign field, because it was too solemn. If God sent men into this work they would be successful. If men sent them they would break down. But he believed there would be fruit. He never had seen a man who expected good results but what he worked so that he secured them. A man who had hope and faith would succeed. The people in this convention all seem to have faith. But they must sink public opinion. They should not look into the papers to see what was said about them. They should not care what the people said. There was no need to make any noise so as to attract attention. It was not always the noisy things that proved successful. There was near his house in the spring, a little brook that went bubbling along over its pebbly surface making a noise all the time, and always making itself known, but when the heat of the summer came the waters of that brook had dried up, and there was nothing left of it. Then, not far away was a great, silent river. He had never heard that river; did not know it was there, because it did not make any noise; but when he found it moving along in its silence, and followed down its course, he found along its banks mills and manufactories that were given power by these waters. We need not blow a trumpet in our work. On a deadwall in Paris there was an inscription which he liked.

It read: "They say. What do they say? Let them say." That was a good motto for Christian workers. They had a work to do, and should go about it, not caring what was said. Should they go forth from this convention to work, or should they let its influence be lost? It was said of Demosthenes that when he spoke the people wanted to go at once to fight with Philip, but when Cicero spoke they went away, saying it was grand. One inspired men to do, the other merely made himself admired. Which should this convention be like? They had had good speeches. Never had he heard better. Never had he seen so much unanimity. Never had he seen Chicago pulpits so well manned as at the present. They were grand men, and were united so that as Dr. Hatfield had said, one could not tell Methodists from Baptists or Presbyterians, or Congregationalists. There was a spirit of unity and he thanked God that these denominational walls had begun to crumble. [Applause.] "Never mind that now. That is not what we want. We want work. Let us go about it. Do all the good you can and work as long as you can."

When he had closed, Mr. Moody stepped back into the crowd on the platform and left the hall at once, taking the evening train for his home in the East.

A hymn was then sung.

Bishop Cheney followed, and reminded the audience that they had not attended the great convention for the pleasurable excitement it had afforded. If they were to turn away from it and say it had been delightful, and enjoyment was the highest thought in their minds, then within thirty days the influence set in motion would be completely lost. Let them realize that the work of the convention was but to set them at work. Though the convention was ended, its work was not done.

Dr. Henson came next with a brief, earnest talk. "What shall we do?" was the question asked. The answer was suggested in the quotation "Whatever thy hand findeth to do." Take what was next your hand. A gift of $10,000 from a rich man might receive the applause of the world, but the music of the widow's mite rose to heaven. It was a grand thing to be a general, and see the battle and hear the shouts of victory, but the life of the private in the ranks was more heroic. Let us be willing to do our little in our little sphere, and let us go down from the high mountain, from this convention into the valley to work. Let us promise to right about face and work. If we could not move great multitudes let us put our hand on the shoulder of some brother and wish that he may become a Christian.

Major D. W. Whittle then exhorted the audience, whether they were Baptists, Episcopalians, Methodists, or Presbyterians, to work together to attain the great object of bringing souls to Jesus. They should not wait until January to hold their revivals; they should engage in the work of saving sinners without delay. A questionable pride kept many away from God. Many of them would find by bitter experience that they had sinful hearts and were in need of God's mercy. If they worked for God and persevered, their end would be glorious. Christ had given His life to save them and they should trust in His ways of redemption.

At his request a large number arose and expressed their willingness to obey God's law. Many also asked for the prayers of the assemblage.

The services were brought to a close by the singing of the "Sweet By-and-by."

THERE'S a land that is fairer than day,
  And by faith we can see it afar;
For the Father waits over the way,
  To prepare us a dwelling-place there.

2 We shall sing on that beautiful shore
  The melodious songs of the blest,
And our spirits shall sorrow no more,
  Not a sigh for the blessings of rest.

3 To our bountiful Father above
  We will offer our tribute of praise,
For the glorious gift of His love,
  And the blessings that hallow our days.

Cho.—In the sweet by-and-by,
    We shall meet on that beautiful shore,
In the sweet by-and-by,
    We shall meet on that beautiful shore.

THE LIFE AND LABORS

—OF—

C. H. SPURGEON,

The faithful Preacher, the Devoted Pastor, the noble Philanthropist, the beloved College President, and the voluminous Writer and Author:

One Elegantly Illustrated Quarto Volume, 650 Pages.

—BY—

GEORGE C. NEEDHAM

Evangelist, Author of " Recollections of Henry Moorhouse," "The True Tabernacle," etc., etc.

THE author says in this preface, "No apology is needed for bringing before our American public, in the present form, the life and labors of this well-known, beloved and faithful minister of Jesus Christ. Mr. Spurgeon has universal fame without seeking it.— Free from selfishness and ambition, and without aiming at popularity, he has enshrined himself in the hearts of thousands and commanded the homage and respect of millions.— His name and labors are interwoven with the religious history of England in the present century; and any one who would acquaint themselves with the great philanthropists of the age, will seek acquaintance with this esteemed pastor."

Mr. Spurgeon has preached for twenty-eight years to a congregation of more than SIX THOUSAND persons, and has now a church whose membership numbers over five thousand. During this long pastorate he has extended the right hand of fellowship to nearly TEN THOUSAND persons. For twenty-seven years his sermons have been published weekly in all parts of the world, and translated into many foreign languages. He has founded and presides over a COLLEGE which is unique in itself, preparing one hundred students for the ministry of the Word; is the originator and director of an ORPHANAGE, giving a home to FIVE HUNDRED needy children. On the twenty-fifth anniversary of his marriage, he gave the testimonial, then given him, of over thirty thousand dollars, to provide an ASYLUM for a score of poor widows.

As a writer, he is the author of over forty different volumes, including Sermons, Commentaries, Lectures and Essays—the sale of one book alone,—" John Ploughman's Talk," having reached a sale of over *three hundred thousand* copies in England. He is also editor of a monthly magazine—"The Sword and the Trowel;" besides, he has started and still watches over many other works too numerous to mention.

Mr. Spurgeon's Life and Example

Will be an incentive to Christian workers, quickening their faith, inflaming their zeal, and encouraging their hearts in labor for the Lord. In reading his thrilling words, the faint-hearted will find encouragement, despondency and unbelief will give place to hopefulness and faith. All weary toilers for God, missionaries, pastors, evangelists, students, and all who in the battle have had more than ordinary trials, will thank God for this noble example, and take courage.

This is a timely book,—the bold, clear, faithful teaching of this great preacher, will in some measure counteract the ill-balanced, weakly, and sentimental theories afloat, as well as deliver from unscriptural, hurtful and skeptical preaching,—now, alas! so general—many disciples of Jesus.

To the thousands of families throughout the country who are isolated from churches, or who may be surrounded by heretical teachers, and who prefer to spend the Lord's day at home, than to allow themselves or children to receive spiritual damage through corrupt doctrine—this work will be doubly welcome, as it will supply interesting, moral and healthful reading. The story of Mr. Spurgeon's life, the peculiarities of his ministry, the history of his Orphanage and College, besides the reports given of the various features of his labors, cannot fail to command interest.

MERCHANTS AND BUSINESS MEN

Who need a book which will not fail to beguile the tedious hours of relaxation—a book which must not be dull or mischievous in its tendencies, will find chapters in this volume FROM HIS PEN which outrival for pure wit and homely wisdom any work extant. Never vulgar, sensual or trifling, the humor of Mr. Spurgeon brings diversion and help and hope with it. His "TALKS" are full of sound advice, keen satire, kindly suggestions, and friendly warnings. No weary man can spend an hour reading these pithy sayings without feeling rested and benefited.

The AUTHOR'S British training, and personal acquaintance with Mr. Spurgeon and knowledge of his labors, peculiarly fit him to write this great work. He is an ENTHUSIASTIC admirer of the great London preacher, and has had free access to the private and public papers of Mr. Spurgeon, and has produced a book which will furnish pleasure and profit and have the fullest approval of one's conscience and judgment—a judgment which will SHARPEN THE INTELLECT, FEAST THE SOUL, AND QUICKEN THE WHOLE MAN.

MINISTERS, LAY PREACHERS, BIBLE READERS AND ALL STUDENTS will find this work a mine of valuable information and suggestion. No book has ever been published containing so much of the GREAT PREACHER and HIS LIFE AND LABORS.

ILLUSTRATIONS.

The Illustrations in this book, over forty in number, have been produced at great expense, made expressly for this work by an ARTIST who has proved to be one of the best of our American artists. The mechanical part of the book is beyond criticism, being done by the Cambridge University Press—the oldest and best in America.

DESCRIPTION AND PRICES.

"The Life and Labors of C. H. Spurgeon" is published in one large square octavo volume, of 650 pages, printed from clear new type, on fine, tinted, heavy crown plate paper, made expressly for this book, and illustrated with a fine, lifelike portrait of Mr. Spurgeon, and forty engravings. It is bound in the most elegant and substantial manner, side stamps in black and gold, of beautiful designs, and is furnished to subscribers at the following prices:

$4.00 .. in Olive **Green Cloth, Plain Edge, Silk Pattern. Beveled Board.**
$4.75 .... in **Olive Green Cloth. Gilt Edge, Green Pattern, Beveled.**
$6.50 .... in **Half Turkey, Antique Back and Marble Edge, Beveled.**

AGENTS WANTED.

The book will be sold exclusively through canvassing agents. In no case will it be sold in bookstores. Active, energetic agents of good character and address, who will canvass closely, will be given specially liberal rates and absolute control of territory, for which commission will be sent on application for outfit. Address for terms

FAIRBANKS, PALMER & CO., Publishers,
133 WABASH AVENUE,
CHICAGO, ILL.

Life and Labors of C. H. Spurgeon.

CHAPTER   I.—INTRODUCTORY.
"   II.—ANCESTRY, PARENTAGE AND BIRTH.
"   III.—CONVERSION AND PREACHING.
"   IV.—CALL TO LONDON.
"   V.—ABUNDANT IN LABORS.
"   VI.—REVIVALS.
"   VII.—MULTIPLYING WORK.
"   VIII.—RESULTS OF OVERWORK.
"   IX.—TRIALS AND DELIVERANCES.
"   X.—DEVISING LIBERAL THINGS.
"   XI.—THE METROPOLITAN TABERNACLE.
"   XII.—THE PASTOR'S COLLEGE.
"   XIII.—THE PRESIDENT'S REPORT, 1881.
"   XIV.—INAUGURAL ADDRESS.
"   XV.—INAUGURAL ADDRESS (continued).
"   XVI.—STOCKWELL ORPHANAGE.
"   XVII.—ANNUAL REPORT, 1881.
"   XVIII.—THE GIRL'S ORPHANAGE.
"   XIX.—SUNSHINE IN THE HEART.
"   XX.—THE COLPORTAGE ASSOCIATION.
"   XXI.—"THE SWORD AND THE TROWEL."
"   XXII.—EDITORIALS (45).
"   XXIII.—CONTRIBUTED ARTICLES BY MR. SPURGEON.
"   XXIV.—REVIEWS.
"   XXV.—LETTERS.
"   XXVI.—PERSONAL NOTES.
"   XXVII.—JOHN PLOUGHMAN'S "TALKS," AND "PICTURES."
"   XXVIII.—THE BIBLE AND THE NEWSPAPERS.
"   XXIX.—MRS. SPURGEON'S WORK.
"   XXX.—CHARLES SPURGEON.
"   XXXI.—THOMAS SPURGEON.
"   XXXII.—SERMONS.

A VALUABLE BOOK.

The Home Guide.

AN ENCYCLOPEDIA OF ALL THINGS OF EVERY-DAY LIFE.

One Large Octavo Volume

OF FIVE HUNDRED AND TWENTY-FIVE PAGES, ELEGANTLY ILLUSTRATED WITH SIXTY-EIGHT ENGRAVINGS.

THE aim of "THE HOME GUIDE" is to give the very best of all that is to be found in expensive and cumbersome works, in a condensed, compact, cheap and convenient form, dispensing with all unnecessary words which mystify and confuse, sifting the wheat from the chaff of all standard authorities, besides adding much practical and valuable information never before published. After many years of toil, and expenditure of many hundred dollars, writing, collecting, gleaning, condensing, and preparing the work for publication, we take pleasure in presenting this Original and Unique Book, feeling we have accomplished a great task in supplying a want long felt,—one that will be appreciated by the public,—a book long sought, but never before obtainable. A complete guide to every department of the household. The best experience of the past condensed for the practical use of the present. A book every family should have, and having, will not be without. The best ideas of the most advanced economists of the age are compiled for common use in this book. DOMESTIC ECONOMY IN A NUTSHELL. It contains Thousands of Important Facts, Valuable Hints, and Useful Suggestions. It tells

How to Secure a Home.   How to Preserve Health.   How to Save in Furniture.   How to Preserve Many Things.
How to Build a Home.   How to Care for the Sick.   How to Save in Fuel.   How to Make Many Things.
How to Furnish a Home.   How to Live Comfortably.   How to Save in Cooking.   How to Mend Many Things.
How to Decorate a Home.   How to Live Cheaply.   How to Save in Clothes.   How to Make Home Happy.

THE HOME GUIDE is adapted to every range of income. The trite axiom, "Economy is wealth," has a significance for all classes of people. Wealth is found, not in having a large income, but in the possession of a surplus after paying judicious expenditures in living. The man of limited means who has even a small balance in his favor at the end of a year, after meeting the demands upon his purse, is richer han another whose income is ten times greater, but who spends more money than he receives. How to obtain economically the necessaries of the household, at the same time to augment convenience and comfort and enhance the enjoyments of life are among the prominent subjects considered in this work; it indicates wherein true economy consists and how by the minimum of expenditure the maximum of comfort may be secured.

Particular prominence is given to hygiene. The laws which govern life and health receive special attention; the value of a knowledge of essential principles is shown; the benefit of exercise is pointed out; the influence of pure air, wholesome food, and cleanliness is demonstrated, while the departments devoted to domestic medicine are exceedingly useful and valuable, especially in cases of sudden illness or accident. The proper treatment of diseases incident to childhood is one of the most important features of the work, and directions and suggestions are given to enable parents and others to guard against the invasion of disease and death in their homes.

In the choice of a home there is information pertaining to things that are very often overlooked, and evils pointed out which ought specially to be avoided. Those who contemplate building will find in this work suggestions as to the best way of planning a house, taking into account the situatian and circumstances of the individual; the materials to be employed in the construction of houses are not overlooked, nor the manner in which the necessary work should be done.

The surroundings of a dwelling exert much influence upon the pleasures and tastes of its inmates, and THE HOME GUIDE, recognizing this important fact, gives the subject proper attention. So, also, the furnishing and decoration of the home is given the consideration it deserves. Under appropriate heads will be found information relating to furnishing every part of the house, according to the means at command, in the most economical, durable, and pleasing manner, as to material, shape, texture and color The portions  relating to ornamentation include some of the simplest methods of rendering the home attractive, a knowledge of which enables the inmates, however humble, to find pleasure and gratification for their ingenuity and taste.

 There are departments also relating to window gardening and the care of house plants, as well as to other branches of rural taste, which contain facts and suggestions that every one may read with profit. The subject of Home Recreation and its influence upon the family is considered from a practical stand-point, and the utility of combining instruction with amusement, and enjoyment with health.

In the preparation of the HOME GUIDE, the especial object has been to produce a work such as is required by the masses; a compendium of useful knowledge of such value that its practical economic, and hygienic features shall recommend it as a useful book in every family; an Encyclopedia of Social and Domestic Economy, which shall be a necessity in every home. It places within the reach of all, at small expense, a fund of information which otherwise must be obtained by long and wearisome experience, or gleaned from an expensive library.

This is a brief outline only of the plan and purpose of THE HOME GUIDE. To attempt even an epitome of its contents in this connection is impracticable within appropriate limits. The work is comprehensive in scope, and full in detail — a *Guide* in fact, as in name, for every department of the HOME.

DESCRIPTION AND PRICES.

"THE HOME GUIDE" is published in one large octavo volume of 526 pages, printed from clear, new type, on fine, tinted, heavy paper, made expressly for this book, and illustrated with 68 engravings. It is bound in the most substantial and elegant manner, beveled board, side stamps in black and gold; of beautiful designs, and is furnished to subscribers at the following prices:

In English Cloth, Back and Side in Black and Gold, $2.00
    "   "   Gilt Edges, "   "   "   2.50
In Arabesque Morocco, Library Style, - - - - 2.75

Agents Wanted!

The book will be sold exclusively through canvassing agents. In no case will it be sold in book stores. Active, energetic agents of good character and address, who will canvass closely, will be given specially liberal rates and absolute control of territory, for which commission will be sent on application for outfit. Address, for terms,

FAIRBANKS, PALMER & CO., Publishers,

133 Wabash Avenue, Chicago, Ill.

SONG PILGRIMAGE

Around and Throughout the World.

By PHILIP PHILLIPS.

INTRODUCTION BY Rev. J. H. VINCENT, D. D.

BIOGRAPHICAL SKETCH BY
REV. ALEXANDER CLARK, D. D.

One Elegant Illustrated 12 mo Volume.
Nearly Forty full page Engravings.

Books of travel have increased of late years almost in the direct ratio to the increased facilities for journeying, and it may be said that the quality has also proportionately improved. The work we now offer the public covers a field and subject contained in no other volume published. SONG PILGRIMAGE embraces a life of song experiences, impressions, anecdotes, incidents, persons, manners, customs, sketches and illustrations throughout twenty different countries visited by the singing pilgrim, Philip Phillips, in his "tour of the world."

In September, 1874, Mr. Phillips left his home in New York, with his family, for the purpose of fulfilling an engagement to sing *one hundred nights* in Australia, and with a view of proceeding from thence round the world. He was able to carry out his intentions, and without an accident of any kind, traveled over *forty thousand* miles and held nearly *six hundred* song services, fulfilling every engagement as advertised. This tour occupied three years' time. The interest in this book is further enhanced by a fine steel plate portrait of Philip Phillips and a large number of others, illustrative of the scenes through which he passed. The world has known the author as one of the most popular solo singers of sacred songs in the world. In this interesting book we find him excelling in a new character, as a careful observer, a thoughtful and patient traveler, and a diligent student of the history, associations, social customs, governmental methods and policies of the countries through which he passed, told in a style both fresh, sparkling and critical. The descriptions are graphic and pictorial. The subjects will be found of permanent interest to all who have a taste for narratives of travel, or would like to follow the author in his unprecedented and enthusiastic tour. We feel confident that the book will prove a valuable acquisition to every private or public library.

The AUTHOR needs no introduction from us. The *millions* of hearts that have been quickened by the sacred songs from the lips of Philip Phillips, will give *all hail* to this volume of the sweetest of all themes of earth or heaven,—the song service of the Lord's redeemed. In the preface to the book the author says:

"The reader will find, in pursuing this record of an itinerant evangelist song, a strangely guided career. That the simple songs of salvation, through the blood of the Lamb, should be heralded along the highways, through the populous cities, across the distant seas, into the remote islands, along the shores of heathen continents, throughout the centers of population in Hindostan, Egypt, the desolations of the Holy Land, and on the continent of Europe, ever and everywhere speaking the same sweet story

'Of Jesus and His Love,'

with crowds attent in every land, tears responding from the faces of aliens and barbarians, strangers and foreigners, with humanity at large, of all tongues and kindreds and tribes, at once glad hearted at the sound of gospel salvation, is, indeed, a wonder of sovereign grace. The health of the singer was marvelously protected all the long journey; his voice never failing, his spirits never desponding, his hopes never flagging and his faith never wavering from the hour of his departure from home until the hour of his return. In this vast schedule of engagements all were fulfilled as advertised; never was the singer late, never disappointed in having an audience. It was a wonderful manifestation, from beginning to end, of the goodness and mercy of God. At every step and in every nation was clearly indicated the divine favor resting upon the effort to reach the world's remotest ear by the voice of singing and the song of redeeming love."

This is Mr. Phillips' first and *only* book, other than sacred song books—the aggregate of the latter having reached the unprecedented sale of nearly Six Million Copies, and have been translated into nearly every language on the face of the globe.

Mr. Phillips stands forth as the pioneer solo singer of sacred song; others have taken to his style of singing, and their names have become household words throughout the English speaking world. The words of no other composer and singer of sacred song were ever before carried by so many types, or carried so far. No other singer addresses so many constantly. He has the *Civilized World* for a congregation

The Illustrations in this book are a *decided feature*, and include inside views of some of the most prominent halls and churches in foreign countries, notably the native churches of India, etc. They are full page wood-cuts, splendid designs, elegantly engraved, and printed on super-calendered, tinted paper, designed and drawn by our best artists, and all illustrative of the subjects.

DESCRIPTION AND PRICES.

"Song Pilgrimage" is published in one large octavo volume, of nearly 500 pages, printed from clear, new type, on fine, tinted, heavy paper, made expressly for this book, and illustrated with a fine, life-like portrait of Philip Phillips, and thirty-two full-page illustrations. It is bound in the most substantial and elegant manner, side stamps, in black and gold, of beautiful designs, and is furnished to subscribers at the following prices:

In English Cloth, Back and Side in Black and Gold, $2.00
In English Cloth, Gilt Edges,   "   "   "   "   2.50
In Turkey Morocco, Gilt Edges, Presentation Edition, 3.50

The Publishers guarantee the book to correspond in every respect with the Prospectus, and unless it does, those who order the work will be under no obligations to take it.

Mailed post paid on receipt of price,

FAIRBANKS, PALMER & CO.,

133 WABASH AVENUE,

CHICAGO, ILL.

It is a man's duty to have books. A library is not a luxury, but one of the necessities of life.---H. W. Beecher.

THE MASQUE TORN OFF

By T. DeWitt Talmage, D. D.,

Author of "Crumbs Swept Up," "Around the Tea Table," "Abominations of Modern Society," "Sports that Kill," etc, etc.

ONE LARGE OCTAVO VOLUME,

OF NEARLY FIVE HUNDRED PAGES, ELEGANTLY ILLUSTRATED WITH ABOUT FIFTEEN FULL PAGE ENGRAVINGS.

THE MASQUE TORN OFF contains the discourses—as lately delivered in the Brooklyn Tabernacle—giving Dr. Talmage's experience and observations, as lately seen by him—in company with two elders of his church and three high police officials—during their midnight explorations in the haunts of vice of New York City. They have been *revised by him for this work*, and are written in his strongest descriptive powers—sparkling with graceful images and illustrative anecdotes, terrible in their earnestness—uncompromising in his denunciation of sin and wickedness wherever found, sparing neither friend nor foe, rich nor poor. Every page of intense interest. No one can read this work without taking new interest in the subjects treated.

CONTENTS.—The work contains nearly FORTY CHAPTERS—on as many subjects—and are Dr. Talmage's best efforts in his earnest, aggressive warfare upon the foes of society, and the exposure of the traps and pitfalls that beset the youth of our land in every city. He sounds a *note of warning*, and points out the ONLY WAY to escape these pits of darkness and social and moral ruin.

THE AUTHOR.—REV. T. DEWITT TALMAGE was born on the 7th of January, 1832, in the village of Bound Brook, New Jersey The story of his life is very simple. A Christian in his teens, a graduate of New York University (1853); a graduate of New Brunswick Seminary; three years a pastor at Belleville, N. J.; three more at Syracuse, N. Y.; seven more at Philadelphia, and now about ten years in Brooklyn,—this is the simple outline of his life. Age has not told on him, though he is not a handsome man. He is not characteristically a graceful man. He is long-limbed and loosely put together. But he is a man of wonderful magnetism—whatever that may be. He *draws*, not merely as an orator, but as a man. He is a man of intense vitality, and intense convictions. This vitality is so superabundant that he easily supplies others with life. His imagination is sensuous and vivid. He sees the external reality of things, and paints them with wonderful pictorial power. That he is a man of unwonted devotion and earnestness, this single illustration must suffice:

Mr. Talmage was pastor of a wealthy and prosperous church in Philadelphia. He was called simultaneously to three churches, one in San Francisco, one in Chicago, one in Brooklyn. That in Brooklyn was poor; it was on the eve of dissolution; it possessed but nineteen male members; its need was greatest, its power was least. Need drew more strongly than strength, and to Brooklyn Mr. Talmage went. For fifteen months he preached to crowded houses. Then the time came to build anew. Mr. Talmage believed in free pews. He emphasized his belief by his action; he relinquished his salary, released his trustees from all pecuniary obligations, trusted himself to a free gospel for his support, and has lived by it ever since.

Mr. Talmage has written several popular books, and his sermons have been published in book form in all parts of the English speaking world, and have reached a sale of great magnitude—75,000 copies of his "Crumbs

Swept Up" being sold in this country alone. Twenty-three papers in Christendom statedly publish his entire sermons and Friday-night discourses, *exclusive of the dailies of the United States;* that the papers girdle the globe, being published in London, Liverpool, Manchester, Glasgow, Belfast, Toronto, Montreal, St John's, Sidney, Melbourne, San Francisco, Chicago, Boston, Raleigh, New York and many others.

The multiplicity, large results and striking progress of the labors of Dr. Talmage have made the foregoing more of a brief narrative of the epochs of his career than an account of the career itself. Lack of space in a circular requires it. This remains to be said: No other preacher addresses so many constantly. The words of no other preacher were ever before carried by so many types or carried so far. Types give him three continents for a church, and the English-speaking world for a congregation. The judgment of his generation will of course be divided upon him just as that of the next will not. That he is *a* topic in every newspaper is much more significant than the fact of what treatment it gives him. Only men of genius are universally commented upon.

ILLUSTRATIONS.—The illustrations in this book are a *decided feature*, and are full page, splendid designs, elegantly engraved, and printed on super-calendered, tinted paper, and designed by Frank Beard, and other artists, illustrative of its subjects.

DESCRIPTION AND PRICES

"The Masque Torn Off" is published in one large octavo volume, of nearly 500 pages, printed from clear, new type, on fine, tinted, heavy paper, made expressly for this book, and illustrated with a fine, life-like portrait of Dr. Talmage, and fourteen full-page illustrations. It is bound in the most substantial and elegant manner, side stamps, in black, red and gold, of beautiful designs, and is furnished to subscribers at the following prices:

In English Cloth, Back and Side in Black, Red and Gold, - - $2.00
"   "   "   Gilt Edges, "   "   "   "   "   "   2.50

Mailed post paid on receipt of price. Address the publishers of this book.

A BOOK FOR EVERY HOME.

BRIGHT AND HAPPY HOMES.

A HOUSEHOLD GUIDE AND COMPANION.

Containing the choicest treasures of Wisdom, Instruction, Amusement and Devotion, original and selected, embracing Marriage, The Home, Husband and Wife, Father and Mother, The Children, The Government of the Home, The Etiquette of the Home, The Æsthetics of the Home, Education in the Home, The Home and the School, The Home and the College, Amusements in the Home, Technical Instructions in the Home, Religion in the Home, Sickness in the Home, Death in the Home, Home and Heaven. Also, a Manual of Amusing and Interesting Experiments in Chemistry and Natural Philosophy, Fascinating Arithmetical Questions and Puzzles, Entertaining Games, and Sleight-of-Hand Performances for the Play-Room and the Parlor, Instruction for Young People in the Use of Woodworking Tools, with Specific Directions for making articles of Beauty and Utility.

By PETER PARLEY, Jr.

WITH AN INTRODUCTION BY

THE RT. REV. SAMUEL FALLOWS, D.D.

One Elegantly Illustrated Quarto Volume.—One Thousand Engravings.

The author of this volume has gleaned from many inviting fields a large portion of the material for a work which, in many particulars, has never been attempted before. The topics under which the accumulated riches of thought and expression have been arranged, are fruitful in suggestiveness. They have been sufficiently amplified to make the work a THESAURUS OF HOUSEHOLD WISDOM.

Bishop Fallows well says: " No human names thrill and stir us like the lyric names of CHILD, MOTHER, and HOME. None contain such a wealth of affection, or such elements of tender remembrance. None bind us so closely to the law of duty, and to the law of love None bring Heaven so near, and make it so real. No work, therefore, can be more important than an earnest and well-directed effort to make the homes of our country BRIGHT AND HAPPY."

DESCRIPTION AND PRICES.

" BRIGHT AND HAPPY HOMES" is published in one large royal quarto volume, printed from clear, new type, on fine, tinted, heavy, extra super-calendered paper, made expressly for this book, finely illustrated and bound in the most substantial and elegant manner, side stamps in black and gold, of beautiful designs, and furnished to subscribers at the following prices:

**In English Silk Cloth Back and Side, in Black and Gold,
Sprinkled Edges**..$4 50
In English Cloth Back and Side, in Black and Gold, Gilt Edges, 5 25
In Full Russia, Presentation Edition, Gilt Edges.................... 7 50
Mailed post paid on receipt of price.

FAIRBANKS, PALMER & CO.,
133 Wabash Ave.,
CHICAGO.

www.ingramcontent.com/pod-product-compliance
Lightning Source LLC
Chambersburg PA
CBHW020248170426
43202CB00008B/281